# The Next Wave

# The Next

An Anthology of 21st Century

Canadian Poetry

# Wave

Edited by Jim Johnstone

Edited by Jim Johnstone
Cover design by Erica Smith
Typeset by Erica Smith

Palimpsest Press would like to thank the Canada Council for the Arts, and the Ontario Arts Council for their support of our publishing program. We also acknowledge the assistance of the Government of Ontario through the Ontario Book Publishing Tax Credit.

*Library and Archives Canada Cataloguing in Publication*

The next wave : an anthology of 21st century Canadian poetry / Jim Johnstone.

ISBN 978-1-926794-70-9 (softcover)

1. Canadian poetry (English)—21st century.
I. Johnstone, Jim, 1978-, editor

PS8293.1.N496 2018          C811'.608          C2017-907126-2

Printed and Bound in Canada by Rapido Books
Fourth Printing

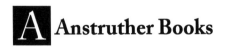

# Contents

# Introduction

Imagine you're invited to a party. You arrive at the venue, slip past security, and Margaret Atwood is there; so are Michael Ondaatje, Anne Carson, and Dionne Brand. CanLit's luminaries surround you, and having never brushed elbows with so many prominent writers, you turn paparazzi and start taking photographs in earnest. Point and click—easy to tell who monopolizes the spotlight and who falls back. It's only once you focus manually, looking for an unconventional angle, that you begin to notice others: a younger, more anonymous crowd pushing at the margins, trying to bypass the guest list. So you raise your camera to include them too, at least those close enough to see clearly. Some of the shots will turn out perfectly—balanced composition, candid expressions that capture the palpable energy of the event. Some won't. The blur of time will seep in, poor exposure rendering the photographs unusable.

You might think I'm describing a Griffin Poetry Prize gala. I am, of course, but this is also the plight of prospective anthologists. Working without the benefit of hindsight, anthologists are responsible for scouting talent in little magazines, hard-to-find books, and critical periodicals. Canonization is a gamble, and time and time again Canadian editors have either gone all in or hedged their bets, offering up both generation defining compilations and remixed versions of established texts. With *New Provinces*, F.R. Scott curated the first essential anthology of Canadian poetry in 1936. Providing a platform for future icons like E.J. Pratt and A.M. Klein, *New Provinces* opened the door for the litany of volumes that followed, including A.J.M. Smith's *The Book of Canadian Poetry* (1943), Raymond Souster's *New Wave Canada* (1966), Gary Geddes's *15 Canadian Poets* (1970), Al Purdy's *Storm Warning* (1971), and Margaret Atwood's *New Oxford Book of Canadian Verse in English* (1982). Despite the relative homogeneity of the writers and work chosen for these anthologies, they were all landmarks in their day, minting names that pushed the country's poetry to commercial heights.

Though CanLit is no longer conceived as the national project it once was in the mid-20th century, the mythology of that era persists. The books mentioned above loom large in the Canadian literary imagination, and it's important to acknowledge that, even in the canon's more recent incarnations, women, Indigenous authors, writers of colour, those with disabilities, and members of the LGBTQ+ community are underrepresented. Slow to evolve, and endemic enough to prevent meaningful change, many major Canadian anthologies are therefore bogged down by the very same books that once propped the nation's literature up. As Shane Neilson asserts in "Canon Confessions," today's poets are hesitant "to acknowledge the value of the canon because of its exclusionary history,"[1] and after the canon wars of the 1980s and 1990s—as well as more recent debates waged over literary nationalism, cultural appropriation and intersectionality—the idea of a single canon does seem prohibitive, if not antiquated. If one were to gather the poets in F.R. Scott's *New Provinces* for example—in the same spirit as Scott himself while satirizing an earlier generation in "The Canadian Authors Meet"—the diversity of the playing field would evaporate, revealing a who's who that remains characteristic of Western literature.

Still, despite skepticism among new generations of Canadian writers, anthologies persist. This is due, in part, to the rise of counter-canons, which provide present-day anthologists with an opportunity to offer alternatives to the country's formative texts. Though representation continues to be uneven, volumes devoted to geography, ethnicity, and sexuality mean that more voices from historically excluded communities are being heard on a national level, contributing to an ever-expanding range of tastes. This upturn is evident in several anthologies published in the new century, from *Native Poetry in*

*Canada* (2001), to *Seminal: The Anthology of Canada's Gay Male Poets* (2007), to the first ten volumes of the *Best Canadian Poetry in English*, all of which reflect an intrepid, boundary-crossing wave of Canadian hopefuls. These hopefuls are also wading into international waters, as the recent publication of *Modern Canadian Poets* (2010) by Carcanet, a major UK-based publishing house, attests.

The reasons for optimism about the future of Canadian poetry do not end with its pluralism. *Breathing Fire 2*, *The New Canon*, and *Open Field*—three of the most lauded Canadian anthologies of last twenty years—all arrived between 2004 and 2005, staking claims for what Carmine Starnino called an "alternative present."[2] Gathered primarily on the basis of the age of the poets included, these surveys use birth dates to consider overarching shifts in subject matter and rhetoric. At the time, a wealth of talent competed for inclusion—over 300 poets submitted work to *Breathing Fire 2*[3]—and Canada's poetry scene has only grown in the years since. Indeed, as of 2016, a greater number of poetry books are being published on a yearly basis than at any point in the country's history.[4] The twenty-first century has ushered in more of everything—MFA programs, small presses, online literary journals—tacitly bolstering Canada's publishing infrastructure and ensuring that this surge of new writing will continue for the foreseeable future.

So why *The Next Wave*? For one, more than ten years have passed since the last major survey of early-to-mid-career Canadian poets was published in Canada. The intervening decade has been a period of rapid change, and *The Next Wave* is designed to bridge the gap by summarizing and expanding the national conversation around poets who now form a distinct, and increasingly accomplished group of writers. Before this happens though, that group needs to be defined. For the purposes of *The Next Wave*, the poets included are:

- Those who have published between one and three trade collections of poetry

- Those who published their first books after 2001

- Those published on all available imprints besides Palimpsest Press

These conditions make *The Next Wave* an output-based anthology, favouring recent work over age-related productivity. They also reward patience. Writers who've held out for quality over quantity—like Sonnet L'Abbe, who has released one full-length collection of poetry since her debut marked the millennium—are represented alongside some of Canada's most essential emerging authors.

In "Canadian Poetry's Unlikely Renaissance," Russell Smith writes that "there hasn't been so much challenging work around – so much that is playful, amusing, dazzling or simply exasperating—for as long as I can remember."[5] While editing *The Next Wave*, I pursued poems with these qualities, insisting on both formal and aesthetic engagement. I also prioritized detail: attention to structure, sonic acuity, and emotional resonance. As an editor who has spent years promoting Canadian poetry, first in *Misunderstandings Magazine*, and more recently at Anstruther and Palimpsest Press, I have seen the skillset of Canada's finest practitioners sharpen. On the ground floor, the gap between form and content has closed, slowly allowing the nation's poets to experiment in ways that were unheard of in the 1980s or 1990s. Take Shane Book's staccato, rhythmically-lineated "Mack Daddy Manifesto," which plays on the conventions of modern hip-hop. This is poetry that relies on improvisation, hammering out a filigreed "gold leaf history" that sounds discordant when placed beside Amanda Jernigan's exacting lyrics, or Ian Williams's nimble, pronoun-rich villanelles and triolets. Discordance, or more pointedly, the vigour of difference, is what connects the poems in *The Next Wave*, revealing contemporary Canadian poetry to be a sort of catch all, extemporized medium.

Although the above might suggest that post-millennial CanLit is still in a transitional phase, the new century has kindled verse that parallels, and draws upon current trends in film and music. It's easy to see the jump cuts in Liz Howard's "Terra Nova, Terraformed" for example, or hear the pop song playing behind Nick Thran's "Earworm." While the diversity of the work available for the anthology made curation difficult, it also forced me to consider each poem within the tradition of the canon as a whole (Canadian or otherwise), rather than holding out for systematic indicators of merit. Sonnet L'Abbe explains her own approach to this challenge in her introduction to *The Best Canadian Poetry in English 2014*:

The kind of curation I want to practice, here and elsewhere, is less about holding new work up against a set of performance indicators and measuring, and more about being able to recognize and celebrate the way new work takes up values indicated by the genre's conventions. Genre is the frame that allows us to talk about writing without simply saying, "It's all poetry! Ergo it's all wonderful"… Calling a work a poem, then, guarantees nothing about its form, suggests little about any rules of execution it might follow, but rather invites us to appreciate the writing for doing, or consciously challenging, things that poetry has traditionally done well.[6]

New Canadian poetry is not easily characterized, and the members of *The Next Wave* both draw on, and demur against, poetic tradition. One need look no further than Jordan Abel, who opens the anthology with fragments of verse repurposed from American western novels, to see this concept in action. Technically, Abel's work can be classified as found poetry, but his redeployment of colonial language is also sui generis, emphasizing how racism is used as justification for the theft of Indigenous land. The texts featured here, *Un/inhabited* and *Injun*, are complex and disorienting, positioning Abel at the forefront of Canada's evolving literary landscape.

Within that landscape, those selected for *The Next Wave* represent the selfie generation. Both self-possessed and self-styled, the majority of the writers in this group harness the echo chamber of the Internet into a malleable, impressionistic music. Scroll through the anthology and you'll find poems like Daniel Scott Tysdal's playful, *MAD Magazine*-inspired "A►◄B" shifting shape alongside formal masterworks like Linda Besner's "Villeneuve Villanelle." You'll also find self-portraits selected from the surfeit of existential poems underpinning twenty-first century CanLit. These include Aisha Sasha John's "Self-Portrait Cemetery," Evan Jones's "Self-Portrait with Argus the Hundred-Eyed," and Sheryda Warrener's "Self-Portrait: *Cassiopeia 1*" and "Self-Portrait: *Nimbus II, 2012*," all of which expose enigmatic personas in a way that modern technology has refreshed. In James Arthur's "Distracted by an Ergonomic Bicycle," he writes:

I felt not only *not myself,*
but that I'd never been… that I

was that man I hardly saw, hurling myself
into the blast, and that everything
I passed—dog, rain, cold, the other guy—
I left in my wake, like afterbirth.

This description of being born anew, of hurtling into a blast catalyzed by everything that the author passes, exemplifies how Canadians are redefining themselves. The early 2000s were a time of empiricism, with artists feverishly evaluating their ideals in relation to evolving cultural trends, and the pervading sense of disaffection from that period has only grown stronger. When Michael Prior states "I am all that is wrong with the Old World / and half of what troubles the New," touching on the racist tendencies that linger not only in Canada, but also worldwide, he challenges the status quo. Others, like Leah Horlick, Sachiko Murakami, and Soraya Peerbaye bolster that ars poetica, answering back with poems that confront and defy structural violence and discrimination.

In his groundbreaking collection of essays, *A Lover's Quarrel*, Carmine Starnino asserts that "any poetry intending to make a case for its importance beyond its own borders needs to show some ability to travel."[7] Like Michael Prior, several of the poets in *The Next Wave* are ex-pats, living and publishing in the United States and overseas. Suzanne Buffam, Chad Campbell, Evan Jones, James Pollock, and Johanna Skibsrud are among those who currently live and work abroad, and several others have published work in major international periodicals like *The Believer, The New Yorker, The Nation, Poetry,* and *PN Review.* Canadian poetry is undoubtedly extending its reach, due in part to the cosmopolitanism of its practitioners. Historically, cosmopolitanism has been used as a marker of national ambition, famously advocated by A.J.M. Smith. In *The Book of Canadian Poetry,* Smith proposed that:

> Some of the poets have concentrated on what is individual and unique in Canadian life and others upon what it has in common with life everywhere. The one group has attempted to describe and interpret what is essentially and distinctively

Canadian… The other, from the very beginning, has made
a heroic effort to transcend colonialism by entering into the
universal.[8]

The difference between today's Canadian poets and those discussed above
is that prevailing notions of cosmopolitanism are no longer tied to national
identity. In an environment where technology is ubiquitous, it is impossible
to ignore how widespread access to information has made global concerns
more immediate. Accordingly, the polarities that Smith posits between artists
invested in "Canadian" virtues and those looking outwards for inspiration
are now anachronisms. While the desire to publish abroad is not new, as *The
Book of Canadian Poetry* makes clear, the poets in *The Next Wave* do so with
greater consistency (nearly every author in the anthology has been published
or reviewed internationally) and less solipsism than in the past. Thanks in
large part to new media, Canadian poetry travels on its own terms, free from
the notion that it is inextricably tied to the place where it was written.

As a result of CanLit's current global mindset, the poems in *The Next Wave*
have an empathy and intelligence wrought from engaging with the world at
large. Consider Jacob McArthur Mooney's "The Fever Dreamer," a monologue
from the perspective of Robert Baden Powell, a British-Army officer who
formed the Boy Scout Association in 1910, or Alexandra Oliver's haunting
childhood tale about a former Nazi party member, "Party Music." While both
are dialectic meditations on inherited trauma, these pieces succeed on their
cultural awareness and adaptability. Then there's Nyla Matuk's "I Declared
My Ethnicity," which links personal ancestry to broader social concerns:

> My origin story involves merchants plying
> between ports of call across the Mediterranean,
> one more arousing than the next. I looked into a mirror
> and saw the Portuguese girl. I declared
> my ethnicity on my latest biographical note, only
> to reap what I so forthrightly did sow.
> Do I look artificial in this mask, I ask.
> You'd mention it in the 1970s, and they'd say terrorist.
> You'd mention it in the 1980s, and they'd say terrorist.
> You'd mention it any old time and they'd assume

a portion of white where there was none.

History is fluid in this passage. Highlighted by the poem's temporal elasticity, Matuk's protagonist adopts multiple selves, mostly from a dissociated viewpoint. All of this clouds the setting in "I Declared My Ethnicity," as if place is amorphous—everywhere and nowhere, simultaneously. Reviewing Matuk's first book, *Sumptuary Laws*, Stewart Cole praised her as "a true citizen of the world" due to "her subjects, settings, and even diction,"[9] and this speaks to the flexibility of her poetics. It also speaks to how Canadians have embraced a global outlook in their work—not as a reaction against literary nationalism, but on the assumption of talent and ability.

Matuk is one of eleven poets from *The Next Wave* who also appeared in the "New Canadian Poetry" portfolio in the December 2017 issue of *Poetry* magazine. Like many contemporary publications, *Poetry* is available free of charge on the web, and resources like the Poetry Foundation's digital archives give instant access to aspiring writers looking to research their craft. Content is pervasive on the Internet, and this has not only altered how information is vetted and shared, but how it is being created. One need only look to the click-bait headlines and fake news sites overtaking traditional news outlets for an example of this type of change in action. Whether from cause or effect, attention spans have diminished, and successful writers have evolved to exploit the urgency of the net—poets included. Poetry relies on associative movement to distinguish it from other forms of writing, and the digital age rewards poets who have learned to leverage lexical devices to supercharge their work. Speed is of the essence, and the poems in *The Next Wave* often break down in the midst of complex thought before reforming with altered internal logic. Though there are pitfalls to this strategy, Canadian poets are willing to sacrifice continuity if synergistic shifts mean breaking new ground.

For better or worse, the speed at which information travels has led to a heightened appetite for discovery, and what often amounts to the fetishization of the new—new media, new technology, new poems. Jeff Latosik captures the ambivalence of this mindset in "The Internet" when he writes: "Its aims seemed as elusive as the stock ticker / or why some people stayed in marriages." This is illustrative of the way lively associative movement, here between stocks and marriage, enriches the connective tissue of present-day poetry. Moreover, the poem's restlessness mimics the hermeneutic nature of the net itself:

> Then, as if an indigenous strain moving beyond a range map,
> people started *getting it*, birdsong calling up from basements,
> the pink noise, hiss, and crackle of a connection made.
> And somebody already had some pictures: the body,
> pixelated, bare, with the feeling you were overseeing it,
> moving along the conveyer belt of banner ads.
> Days went by like they were being dragged into a bin.

In this stanza, Latosik channel-surfs between images (a range map, basements, the body, the conveyer belt of banner ads) in an attempt to nail down an experience that's almost ethereal. Many have freighted poems with this kind of lexical uncertainty in the past, but it is the syntactic fluidity of "The Internet" that makes it stand out, enlivening a machine that has taken on a life of its own in popular culture.

Poets like Latosik, who are locked in to the cultural and technological zeitgeist, have helped CanLit settle into a sweet spot where mainstream media meets art. Read on and you'll catch Raoul Fernandes riffing on email etiquette in "Attachments," and Suzanne Buffam listing trendy (and often satirical) annoyances in "First World Problems A to Z." Moreover, you'll notice how the use of simile and metaphor among Canadian poets has become almost telescopic, with multiple levels of meaning spring-loading language. Linda Besner is the epitome of this approach, applying a torqued vernacular, layered analogies, and sudden shifts in momentum to reinforce her subject matter and tone. Here's the opening of "Feel Happier in Nine Seconds":

> I learned the secret of serenity
> by waterboarding daffodils.
> My Buddha is landfill.
> My mantra choked
>
> from a bluebird's neck.
> It's ruthless, the pursuit
> of happiness. Eighteen
> seconds have elapsed.

My happiness is twice
your size, gold-chained
to the lamppost. It strains
its waistcoat as it grows.

Flog a sunbeam, harness
a cloud. You should be feeling
five times happier now:
the world is your Kleenex.

The capricious charm of Besner's diction is a willed construction rather than mere idiosyncrasy. While tallying the time between rapid-fire metaphors, "Feel Happier in Nine Seconds" seesaws, perpetually amending its central theme. Serenity is found when waterboarding daffodils; happiness grows, and after the reader is urged to "Flog a sunbeam," Besner advises that they "should be feeling / five times happier now." This technique finds its origin in repurposed cliché—the likes of which Jason Guriel similarly exploits when he begins the poem "Less" by claiming that less "—cooked by crooked / math—is more / than enough." Both Besner and Guriel, along with Sadiqa de Meijer, Ben Ladouceur, and Johanna Skibsrud, have pioneered poetic practices underscored by an elevated rhetorical intricacy that has become much imitated in Canadian letters.

If *The Next Wave*'s poets are indeed members of the selfie generation, then rhetorical intricacy is akin to a photographer's quest for depth of field. Strikingly, many of the anthology's poems have a photographic quality, with mnemonic language and shape-shifting syntax providing nuance to otherwise common subjects. For example, when Dani Couture's speaker observes the sky from an airplane window in "Contact," describing "Cloud cover like a badly made bed, ruched in sections, rushed," she establishes a secondary reality. Not finished with this comparison, Couture boldly runs with the opening image, trusting the reader to drill deeper until "The gathered duvet sometimes mimics you, / makes double." Personifying the outside world as an "escape route" from the plane, the poet constructs a sort of safe space before depicting a distressing encounter with a fellow passenger. Without its initial analogy, "Contact" would be much less urgent. Instead, as the poem's action moves outwards, Couture's voice intensifies until the moment the aforementioned passenger lifts "his shirt to show you where his lungs had been punctured and once / collapsed." "Contact" is actively cinematic, and one of many instances in *The Next Wave* where an author's signature style results in genuine fervor.

Despite the individual accomplishments that stood out while editing *The Next Wave*, the most surprising aspect of the project is how it evolved over time. I began selecting poets in early-2014; over three years later less than half of my initial picks remained. Shuffling, trading, and re-examining both poems and poets, I became aware of how seamlessly my choices were tied to the moment I made them. This was compounded by *The Next Wave*'s selection criteria, which forced me to select a finish date so that candidates would no longer be able to write themselves in or out of the project. Ultimately, the line-up was locked down in September 2017. In the years the anthology remained in flux however, poets like Darren Bifford, Brecken Hancock, Rachel Lebowitz, Cassidy McFadzean, Robin Richardson, and Moez Surani all stood alongside the authors you're about to read. On any given day, these writers belong in discourse with Canada's best.

Curatorially, *The Next Wave* casts a wide net. Deliberately crafted to break away from the conservative tradition of the canon, the anthology strives to represent the multi-faceted and increasingly changeable state of the Canadian literary community. Accordingly, the poems within are meant as an introduction—a primer that will spur dialogue around the current state of Canadian poetry—not a definitive statement on who's in and who's out. I'm a firm believer in the flexibility of taste, and *The Next Wave* is, at its core, a personal canon. In an interview with the *Montreal Gazette* in 2005, Sina Queyras observed that "a healthy writing community has a lot of different scenes, not exclusive or divisive scenes, but distinct ones, with a lot of crossover."[10] That crossover is where anthologies have the opportunity to intersect, as is already evident by Suzanne Buffam and Joe Denham's presence in *The New Canon* and incarnations of *Breathing Fire* as well as the pages that follow.

Flip forward and you'll discover that the poets in *The Next Wave* now populate the party where this introduction began. Nearly twenty years since the dawn of the millennium, the spotlight that I initially described has turned into a strobe light, touching on a generation currently unsettling the formula for writing "Canadian" poetry. There is a sleight-of-hand to the poems in *The Next Wave*, a legerdemain marshaled by poets attuned to the coincident and strange. Speaking to Amanda Jernigan in *The Partisan* in 2014, Alexandra Oliver praised poetry's ineffability, saying: "Topic doesn't make [a] poem. There has to be the inner rattle, the resonating essence that makes the act [of writing] very urgent."[11] *The Next Wave* celebrates this exigency, establishing a dance floor for writers ushering in a new poetic consciousness. Soon, those who fell outside of the inclusion criteria will find themselves on the verge of crowding in; ready to join the flood of poets in these pages galvanizing the future of Canadian literature.

Jim Johnstone
Toronto, 2017

# Works Cited

1. Neilson, Shane. "Canon Confessions." *Canadian Notes & Queries* 97 (2016): 16-20. Print.

2. Starnino, Carmine. *The New Canon: An Anthology of Canadian Poetry.* Montreal: Véhicule Press, 2005. Print.

3. Crozier, Lorna and Lane, Patrick. *Breathing Fire 2: Canada's New Poets.* Gibsons: Nightwood Editions, 2004. Print.

4. Mooney, Jacob McArthur. "30 After 30 Under 30: a.m. kozak (ed.)'s *30 Under 30*." *Arc Poetry Magazine*, August 11, 2017. Online.

5. Smith, Russell. "Canadian Poetry's Unlikely Renaissance." *The Globe and Mail*, September 19, 2012. Online.

6. L'Abbe, Sonnet. *The Best Canadian Poetry in English 2014.* Toronto: Tightrope Books, 2014. Print.

7. Starnino, Carmine. *A Lover's Quarrel.* Erin, Ontario: The Porcupine's Quill, 2004. Print.

8. Smith, A.J.M. *The Book of Canadian Poetry: a Critical and Historical Anthology.* Chicago: The University of Chicago Press, 1943. Print.

9. Cole, Stewart. "A Review of Nyla Matuk's *Sumptuary Laws*." *The Urge*, October 12, 2012. Online.

10. Swoboda, Victor. "Young writers drive Montreal's literary scene." *Montreal Gazette*, May 8, 2015. Online.

11. "Alexandra Oliver and Amanda Jernigan in Conversation." *The Partisan*, January 12, 2016. Online.

# Jordan Abel

**Jordan Abel** (b. 1985) is a Nisga'a writer from BC. Currently, he is pursuing a PhD at Simon Fraser University where his research concentrates on intergenerational trauma and Indigenous literature. Abel's creative work has recently been anthologized in *Best Canadian Poetry in English* (Tightrope), *The Land We Are: Artists and Writers Unsettle the Politics of Reconciliation* (Arbiter Ring), and *The New Concrete: Visual Poetry in the 21st Century* (Hayword). Abel is the author of *The Place of Scraps* (winner of the Dorothy Livesay Poetry Prize), *Un/inhabited*, and *Injun* (winner of the Griffin Poetry Prize).

## uninhabited

Changing horses frequently, one day
out I had left Red River in my rear, but
before me lay an              country,
unless I veered from my course and went
through the Chickasaw Nation. Out to-
ward Bear Canyon, where the land to the
north rose brokenly to the mountains,
Luck found the bleak stretches of which
he had dreamed that night on the ob-
servation platform of a train speeding
through the night in North Dakota,—a
great white wilderness unsheltered by
friendly forests,              save by
wild things that moved stealthily across
its windswept ridges. This done, they
would lead the ship to an
part of the shore, beach her, and scatter
over the mainland, each with his share
of the booty. How lonely I felt, in that
vast              bush! Except for a
very few places on the Ouleout, and
the Iroquois towns, the region was
          . This was no country for
people to live in, and so far as she could
see it was indeed              . But for the
lazy columns of blue smoke curling up
from the pinyons the place would have
seemed              . It appeared to be
a dry,              forest. In the vivid
sunlight and perfect silence, it had a new,
          look, as if the carpenters and
painters had just left it. It was in vain that
those on board made remonstrances and
entreaties, and represented the horrors

of abandoning men upon a sterile and
island; the sturdy captain
was
inflexible. The herbage is parched and
withered; the brooks and streams are
dried up; the buffalo, the elk and the deer
have wandered to distant parts, keeping
within the verge of expiring verdure, and
leaving behind them a vast
solitude, seamed by ravines, the beds of
former torrents, but now serving only
to tantalize and increase the thirst of the
traveller. It kept on its course through a
vast wilderness of silent and apparently
mountains, without a savage
wigwam upon its banks, or bark upon
its waters. They were at a loss what route
to take, and how far they were from the
ultimate place of their destination, nor
could they meet in these
wilds with any human being to give them
information. They forded Butte Creek,
and, crossing the well-travelled trail
which follows down to Drybone, turned
their faces toward the
country that began immediately, as the
ocean begins off a sandy shore.

# From *Injun*

a)

he played injun in gods country
where boys proved themselves clean

dumb beasts who could cut fire
out of the whitest[1] sand

he played english across the trail
where girls turned plum wild

garlic and strained words
through the window of night

he spoke through numb lips and
breathed frontier[2]


b)

he heard snatches of comment
going up from the river bank

*all them injuns is people first*
*and besides for this buckskin*

*why we even shoot at them*
*and seems like a sign of warm*

*dead as a horse friendship*
*and time to pedal their eyes*

*to lean out and say the truth*
*all you injuns is just white keys*

g)

      injuns in a heap
spring       boiled over

lanterns buried
light against    day

old rifle       old trip
       the doubt outlasted

just cattle dying
a       promise of appetite

of one man owned


o)

injun s      mu  st   hang

         straigh  t
         bl  ack arrows

         o ff their
         sh  oulders

         an d  be     th   ankf  ul
         and b e   faithf ul
         a nd     be   tr  ustful

of si   lver and
     lu  ck

p)


              g
                                   cl    f

       b loody
te  eth
            o
      kr               sc   out

         p aleface          a
n  a
               c                 r

             s


           si   lvertip

             b
               g    e

1)

himself clean strain that night, the **whitest** little Injun on the reserva
s along the Missouri River had the **whitest** lot of officers that it was e
at is spirit. He smiled, showing the **whitest** and evenest teeth. Such e
Jerry wants to talk to you. He's the **whitest** of the lot, if you can call t
d not observe that his teeth are the **whitest**, evenest." "They make th
oked from face to face. "You're the **whitest** bunch—I'd like to know-
't much just to look at, but he's the **whitest** man I ever knew. You wa
ll you see Blanco Sol! Bar one, the **whitest**, biggest, strongest, fastest
el rolls, pure, clean, and sweet, the **whitest** and finest in the world! ,
l her, anyway. Monty Price was the **whitest** man I ever knew. There's
me. Al Auchincloss always was the **whitest** an' squarest man in this s
An' Coles swore thet Wade was the **whitest** man he ever knew. Heart
alousy and be half decent. He's the **whitest** man I ever knew. "Now I
e of Colorado you're known as the **whitest** of the white. Your name's
s with startlin' truth. Wade was the **whitest** man I ever knew. He had

2)

ige. San Antonio at this time was a **frontier** village, with a mixed populatio

s and asked none in return. In this **frontier** village at a late hour one night

ι passing glance. Interesting as this **frontier** life was to the young man, he p

the work before them. There was a **frontier** on the south and west of over t

redit due for guarding this western **frontier** against the Indians and making

he soil, as a boy the guardian of the **frontier** was expert in the use of firearn

nds. In the use of that arbiter of the **frontier**, the six-shooter, they were artis

near to hear him. His years on the **frontier** were rich in experience, though

ave it to the stronger republic. This **frontier** on the south has undergone fev

ιunties in Texas while it was yet the **frontier**, and by industry and economy

in the early days usually graced the **frontier** towns with their presence. This

sinner said that he had been on the **frontier** some little time, and that there

ιat the Ford was quite a pretentious **frontier** village of the squatter type. The

classify him at a passing glance as a **frontier** gambler. As we turned away fro

tern trail. On coming opposite that **frontier** village, Parent and I took the w

ιr another trail drover. Sutton was a **frontier** advocate, alike popular with th

ιd had grown into manhood on the **frontier**. Sponsilier was likewise pleasec

ad herd. It was a unique posse. Old **frontier**smen, with patriarchal beards a

# James Arthur

**James Arthur** (b. 1974) grew up in Toronto. His first book, *Charms Against Lightning*, was published in 2012 by Copper Canyon Press. Arthur's poems have appeared in *The New Yorker*, *The New York Review of Books*, *The London Review of Books*, *Brick*, *Poetry*, *The American Poetry Review*, and *Ploughshares*. He has received the Amy Lowell Travelling Poetry Scholarship, a Hodder Fellowship, a Stegner Fellowship, a Discovery/*The Nation* Prize, and a Fulbright Scholarship to the Seamus Heaney Centre for Poetry in Northern Ireland. Arthur lives in Baltimore, where he teaches in the Writing Seminars at Johns Hopkins University.

## Omnivore

I eat what's put in front of me,
as all great men do. Should you eat shark? I know

some wouldn't, but I do, if it's there.
Scorpions too, and their stingers; swallowing a scorpion

won't poison you. Old-time glue-makers
made glue of old horses, and I

make use when I can.
Someone put his wife in front of me; someone else,

his mediocrity. What I know, I swear by—
feed yourself, or die.

James Arthur

# Distracted by an Ergonomic Bicycle

On a rainy morning in the worst year
of my life, as icy eyelets shelled the street,
I shared a tremor with a Doberman
leashed to a post. We two were all the world
until a bicyclist shot by, riding

like a backward birth, feetfirst,
in level, gentle ease, with the season's hard breath
between his teeth. The rain was almost ice, the sky
mild and pale. I saw a milk carton bobbing by
on a stream of melting sleet.

    *A bicyclist. A bicyclist.* He rode away—
to his home, I guess. I went home,
where I undressed, left my jacket
where it fell, went straight to bed, and slept
for two days straight. But those clicking wheels

kept clicking in my head, and though
I can't say why, I felt not only not myself,
but that I'd never been… that I

was that man I hardly saw, hurling myself
into the blast, and that everything
I passed—dog, rain, cold, the other guy—
I left in my wake, like afterbirth.

## On Day and Night

And as the neighbors' guests retire, coaxing their cars
into the snow (we're gazing through the curtain
into winter's pale hub) two girls gaze up. They're all
going home, like wheels correcting
into steering hands, or drawn breath returning to the air,
but you can't come back to anywhere—there's no perfect here
and there, or now and then—but here we are,
again. A silverfish crosses the windowpane. We peer
into the street, and up at the stranded moon: White wheel,
black field. Black winter, white road. White silence,
black wind. White cars, black wires.

James Arthur

# The Sympathy of Angels

Being of tragic bent
we incline to the future

and the past. But we
see you. We
see how tired you are
as you lean on your rifle

or your shovel.
We see the fired shells
and the head they go into.
We too are shells,
you too are graves.
Equally to all men, we

have nothing to say.
*Adore.* We are just. We
serve a monarch
in a silk sarcophagus.

## A Local History

My grandmother's house was always full of flies.
They'd crawl across each other on the windowsill
or would be spinning out their noisy dying

everywhere, in such number, you could sweep forever
and not get all the dead flies off the floor. Out of the house
and downhill, in a marsh of cattails and bristle-sided reeds,
milkweed pods kept cracking open, leaking seed across the air,
renewing the existence of their species
in the way they'd done from year to year.

Way back when, some hard-handed Methodist pioneer
had somehow wrenched up every stone
big enough to break a plough,
and piled them all throughout the woods,
where they still were, in mounds, when I was growing up:
like barrows heaped above the decomposed remains
of the violent Saxon kings, whose grave-goods
featured large in my imagination.

My grandmother's gone. Before she died, she lost her words,
her house, her name, but for me, she's still a hard old woman
walking downhill at dawn, long into autumn,
to skinny-dip in her weed-choked, freezing pond.
A hedge of wind, a wall of suburban snow—
my father's father's ashes are in the ground
in southern Ontario. Something I read in college
and for whatever reason have not forgotten

is that the Saxon barrow-makers,
living among the wrecks of Roman buildings
they could not copy
or restore, saw themselves as late arrivers, as an *after-folk*
living on the graves of a greater folk
who'd gone before. *Where is the horse, where the rider,*
some now-nameless Saxon wrote,
grieving for a people who his own forebears
had annihilated, assimilated,
or driven into the sea.

# Billy-Ray Belcourt

**Billy-Ray Belcourt** (b. 1994) is from the Driftpile Cree Nation. He is a 2016 Rhodes scholar and a PhD student in the Department of English and Film Studies at the University of Alberta. *This Wound is a World,* his first book, was selected by CBC Books as the best Canadian poetry collection of 2017. Billy-Ray is also a community educator and has taught or is teaching creative writing at The Edmonton Remand Centre and The Learning Centre Literacy Association. A public intellectual, his essays have been published in *Canadian Art, GUTS Magazine, ArtsEverywhere.ca,* and *Decolonization.*

# The Cree Word For a Body Like Mine is Weesageechak

the cree word for a body like mine is *weesageechak*. the old ones know of this kind of shape-shifting: sometimes i sweat and sweat until my bones puddle on the carpet in my living room and i am like the water that comes before new life.

i was born during a falling leaves moon; which is to say that i have always been good at sacrifice. it is believed that women are most powerful during their moontime and because of this do not take part in ceremonies in order to let the body cleanse itself. there are *weesageechak* days when gender is a magic trick i forgot how to perform and my groin floods and floods trying to cleanse itself like the women and i too become toxic for men who have built cages out of broken boys.

maybe if i surrendered myself to grandmother moon she would know what to do with these pickaxe wounds. there is so much i need to tell her about how my rivers and lakes are crowded and narrowing. how i managed to piece together a sweat lodge out of mud and fish and bacteria. she gives me the cree name *weesageechak* and translates it to "sadness is a carcass his tears leave behind."

and the crows and flies who don't care about gender will one day make away with my jet-black finger nails and scraggly armpit hairs. they will lay tobacco at my grave and tell their crow and fly kin that i was once a broad-shouldered trickster who long ago fell from the moon wearing make-up and skinny jeans.

# God's River

*it is september 2009 and health canada sends body bags to god's river
first nation – a community hit hard by swine flu*


a body bag
is a gun
is a smallpox blanket
is a treaty
– call it a medicine chest

wait for
an autopsy
they call it H1N1
you call it
the pass system:
bodies like
these can
only leave if
they're on
stretchers
– call it "moving"

someone says:
"it's like sending
body bags
to soldiers in
afghanistan"

remind them
that canada is
four hundred
afghanistans
– call it colonialism

to live in
trenches like these
is to be
civilian casualty
and soldier all at once
– call it a "suicide epidemic"

wonder
how many deaths
it takes for a
country to
call itself
god

think maybe
reserve is
another word
for morgue
is another word
for body bags
– call it home anyways

## Love is a Moontime Teaching

love is a moontime teaching
is your kookum's crooked smile when you pick up the phone
is another word for body
body is another word for campfire smoke
campfire smoke is the smell he leaves behind in your bed sheets after
the breakup
the word for hate sex is forest
forest sometimes means hope or lonely (depends on who you ask)
lonely is a movie called *taxi zum klo* about white gay men
who risk tiptoeing through desire's minefields
for ten minutes of something better than living
living is going to bingo to pay the bills
after you quit your job that barely paid the bills
paying the bills is sometimes a metaphor for cancer
cancer is a diagnosis handed down to an 18-year old girl from the rez
the rez is another word for body
the body is a myth
is the only good news the doctor gives you when your cells run amok
amok is the border the skin doesn't remember
how to secure anymore
anymore is the feeling you get when a police officer
pulls you over because he thinks you're driving a stolen vehicle
a stolen vehicle is the nickname you give to love.

# Linda Besner

**Linda Besner**'s (b. 1980) second poetry collection, *Feel Happier in Nine Seconds*, was published in 2017 by Coach House Books and shortlisted for the A.M. Klein Award. Her first book, *The Id Kid*, was named as one of the *National Post*'s Best Poetry Books of the Year. Her poetry and journalism have appeared in numerous magazines including *The New York Times*, *The Boston Review*, *The Walrus*, and *Real Life*, and been anthologized in *Best Canadian Poetry 2012*. In 2015 she was selected as one of the Writers' Trust of Canada's best emerging artists. She lives in Montreal, where she is on the editorial board of Icehouse Press.

## Mornings with the Ove Glove™

Encased in the new five-fingered Nomex shield
recently lost to the Space Race and run aground
in the suburbs, I stand before the mirror and soothe
my flyaway hair with the om comb.
In the kitchen, I reify
a slice of toast with am jam, watch
from the window as the neighbourhood id kid
takes one giant leap and clears the fence.
His parents were like everyone, swept up
in the us fuss, advancing the species faster
than the Russians. Hurrying to make their own
clone and send it out there, the latest ape shape
clomping around the garden barefaced as a dartboard.
Back then, I too felt the night ignite
with passion; for a few giddy years
there were fumblings, scaldings, dropped casseroles,
but now I've got a grip. *Five times stronger than steel,*
*look what we can do,* I remind myself,
and dump my coffee dregs down the ink sink,
that fathomless black hole. Heave my Kevlar coat
off the rack and leave for irk
work before the ought rot sets in.
Down the stairs, on the once and future side of the or door,
I see the neighbour girls have abandoned
the nameless secret they were building.
Instead, set up a lawn salon
in their front yard. One girl transforming
the other with I dye, her hatchling boyfriend watching
from the you pew. I think the rocketship wreckage
might still be on fire—that, or maybe
there are hot coals where I'm walking. Yes,
a crack, a crater, and then a glimpse
of the hissing ur-face surface,
the faith test, the scorcher.

But my moonboots are the real thing,
NASA cast-offs. Lately nothing can touch me.
I see the kid again—he's climbed to the top
of the battleship jungle gym across the way
in the ark park, surveys the monkey bars
like an odd god debating flood.
The swings are at autumn
bottom; it's a long countdown to next liftoff.
I fish my keys from my pocket.
Something's missing. Love? A hovercraft,
something to take me ninety miles above I'm time
into the tuneless everblasting in-it minute?
I can thrust my hands straight into the fire,
withstand 450 degrees
of separation, nothing will ever be too far-
fetched again. I bury any uncertainty
in the utter clutter of the I'll file—*Think about this later.*

## Villeneuve Villanelle

A van, verily, *une livraison, l'avenir* arrived *d'ailleurs*, a day
avowed comely, *lueur d'avril* bespoke, bespilled—*ça brille*.
*L'imprévu s'avance* impervious; appears apace, *s'est envolé*.

A novice driver, *évidemment*. One *virage rapide*, and all *bouleversé*,
an avalanche of navel oranges *devant la fruiterie*.
A future in delivery, *vraiment*. Moreover, this arrival—*le camion, la journée*—

*grand événement* for the vagrants pocketing oranges *à volonté*,
*poursuivis* by the vainglorious vendor, *à petit* avail. *Ainsi*,
unforeseen advances; *une apparition imperméable* that *vite* blows away.

*Une idée*, maybe, of ivied-over avenues *à suivre*, asway
with *lilas*, novelistic verandas. *Rossignols*. Lily-of-the-valley.
*En accouchant, l'espoir*. Arriving, *d'ailleurs*, a truck, a day *en vérité*,

a vaudeville on *la rue* Villeneuve: thrown oranges, *oranges lancées*;
flown oranges, *oranges volées*. Runnelling nuance *d'après ceci*:
*une proposition inattendue*; ghost in a raincoat, *échappé*.

Abundance, rolling. *Une voie* beloved *d'agrumes*, ravished by *abeilles*.
And *attendant aux feux*, unbeknownst to driver, fruitman, *sans-abris*:
a van, verily. *Une livraison, l'avenir* arrived *d'ailleurs*—a day
*imprévu s'avance* impervious. Appears apace; then *envolé*.

50

Linda Besner

# Feel Happier in Nine Seconds

I learned the secret of serenity
by waterboarding daffodils.
My Buddha is landfill.
My mantra choked

from a bluebird's neck.
It's ruthless, the pursuit
of happiness. Eighteen
seconds have elapsed.

My happiness is twice
your size, gold-chained
to the lamppost. It strains
its waistcoat as it grows.

Flog a sunbeam, harness
a cloud. You should be feeling
five times happier now:
the world is your Kleenex.

It's been a long sixty-three
seconds in Attawapiskat,
but my happiness digs
diamond mines, slobbers

parasol knobs on the Rhine.
I sweeten my cantaloupe
with stolen breastmilk.
Peak joy is at nine

times nine—saddle up, dear.
An asteroid of happiness
is blasting through
the atmosphere.

## Water Glass

Sure fooled me.
Had me right up
to the tinselly scraping

when I downed
the last mouthful
and the ice cube turned

out to be glass.
Arrowhead.
Shark's fin.

Lifting it out
nearly cost me a finger
never mind

the carnage it
could've caused
in the throat.

Awe around the table
as if I'd gone
inadvertent skydiving

or breezed through
a tiger rodeo just while
sipping, squeezing in

a lime. See
how the trick is turned.
Thrilling to be fooled so,

like when I went to check
the time in Paris
and a thief's hummingbird

caress left me gaping
at my naked wrist.
That was a touch

I never felt, but this time
I'm suffered to see
how I'm spared.

Everyone wanted to touch it, tap,
test their fingers on the edge.
Makes you want

to try your luck again,
the way a carnival bohunkus
gawps at the stage;

then jets his hand
in the air with ballooning
faith. Me, me,

pick me, mister.
Saw me in half.
I believe.

# Shane Book

**Shane Book**'s (b. 1970) first collection, *Ceiling of Sticks*, won the Prairie Schooner Book Prize and the Great Lakes Colleges Association New Writers Award. His second volume, *Congotronic*, won the Archibald Lampman Award and was shortlisted for the Canadian Authors Association Award, Ottawa Book Award, and Griffin Poetry Prize. He is also a filmmaker whose award-winning work has screened at film festivals and on television around the world. He was educated at New York University, the Iowa Writers' Workshop and Stanford University, where he was a Wallace Stegner Fellow. He was the 2016-2017 Writer-in-Residence at the University of Calgary and is now an associate professor in the Department of Writing at the University of Victoria.

# African Evening

I had a thing for mange.
Her skin was fluorescent with it.
The open canoe made smooth, curling sounds.
It smelled like the man I am told is mother.
Mother sped his brain on pills.
He limped.
He gripped mother's leg and begged.
The long open canoe had a wind inside
and a yellow sky and a smell of mother.
I went to the docks to pray.
The trees were yellow, the trees were orange
and her panties had been cut away.
I had a thing for docks and praying on the little bronze pipes.
I stained them with my fluid.
I had a bald thing, a bashed in thing, a thing for her grease.
In my arms I held an end of the long canoe and slit it
sternum-first into the sea.

## Mack Daddy Manifesto

*Ultimately, when stubborn historical facts had dispersed all intoxicating effects of
self-deception, this form of Socialism ended in a miserable fit of the blues.*
   – Karl Marx & Friedrich Engels


A spectre is haunting Europe
but I feel the sun cocooning
in a triple-breasted track suit

         when I think of you. Thus we
         obtain our concept of the unconscious
         from the theory of repression, a sweet finish

after the bitter pills of floggings and bullets,
my Tender-roni, my Maytag Blue –
for real, you like them dresses? I'll bag the whole rack – let
the ruling classes tremble

"But you Communists would introduce
community of women!" screams
the chorus.
         All I'm thinkin' is Sugar,
         African me till you African't
         leave every jaw

         dropped, cocked and locked,
         freeze the whole
         homeboy corner crew:
         Pope - Czar,
         Metternich - Guizot,
         French Radicals - German police spies

all sewing duodecimo editions
of New Jerusalem, this special organ appearing
to be the muscular apparatus of

old Europe's powers
in holy alliance to exorcise

this special organ appearing to need
    my help. I do what I can. "Hola' hotty!" I holla –
    when what I really mean is,
    "Baby got back!" as here
   and there among the spindly trees the contest
   breaks out into riots: What does it mean when we say

making something conscious? Have not
the Christians already declaimed:

*Underneath this thug armor: a corn ear of nuclear cornea fission.*
*It fuels my new clear cornrow vision.*

*All fixed frozen relations,*
*their ancient*
*and venerable trains*
*swept away,*
*all new-forms*
*antiquated before*
*they can ossify?*    Sho' 'nuff,

at fifty feet your party smile puts a wrinkle
in a salt fish patty substitute for longing for the father,
the germ religions spawned. By days, by degrees they
sink into their fanatical, superstitious belief
in the miraculous effects of their social science.
And you thought I was a player
'cause you heard some other guy lace that last line
to your little sister? Little did you know he wasn't nothing
but a biter, player-hating 'cause the ladies
love me despite the fact my hair is nappy—

the annexation taking place as when
a foreign language is appropriated,
namely, by translation—

unlike
"True" Socialism, which appears to kill
with one stone,
spreads like an epidemic,
and is fore-most a body-ego.
Of course this is only hypothesis,
there's no museum space
to offer – exhibit A:

the ever-mean talk show hosts,
bitter preachers, dirty rappers,
all up in my shit,
running their mouths
like they was me,

but winding up lipping blisters:

Whereas the Communists have no need to  introduce
free love; it has existed almost from time
immemorial, and on and on to the break
of dawn, to let us now
take wage labor:

clinical observation showing
circumstances where hate changes to love,
love to hate and

our bourgeoisie taking great
pleasure in seducing each other's wives.
Real real soon,
as in yester-after-noon, I need to step to
your crib, and tell you how I feel the proletarians
have nothing to lose but their world to win.

                                          Be ready chula,
                                      I'm a move the mood up.
                               You gonna call me "Vision master,"

Ergo, those who work, acquire nothing and those who
acquire anything, do not work!

Ain't it all good,
ain't it morning before you know it,
ain't my suits crazy insulated
with gold leaf history

in which free
development of each
is the condition
                    for free development of all.

Likewise it has to feed a man,
instead of being fed to him. He
becomes an appendage of the machine,
but it is only simple yak fur
lining my boots
that I need if I got you...
                    I'll make
                    all that is solid melt into air
                    all that is holy profaned

# Homecoming

Beside me a woman moves her lips
and I wonder if she's praying.
With his stunted machine
gun the checkpoint soldier waves
us down, stilling the drum and creak
of the *tro-tro* bus. In front of me
tightly strapped to a woman in bright
aqua homecoming cloth, a baby
stops gurgling, lays his head
down on her brown back,
closes his eyes. We file out into
a heat and red dust field.
A guardhouse, thin and shaky
like the soldiers, crumbling mud
walls, tin roof half ripped open
like a can of smoked oysters.
From somewhere, more guards
appear, more guns with taped-on
crescent-shaped magazines.
The one who waved us in walks
down the line, stopping at a watch,
shirt collar, face, as though
inspecting troops in the Independence
Day parade. Reeking of palm
wine, he sways and his dented
gun sways. Beside me a woman
moves her lips and I wonder
if she's praying. Someone's got
enough of what the soldiers want
and what is it. From her cloth bag
I smell pepper-smoke, dried fish.
The noon sun hits. Who among us
won't get back on the bus?
Peering at a child's sandals, the soldier

leans over too far, hitting
the red dirt hard. We don't say
anything. Another soldier shouts
and points at the fallen man
and the soldiers all laugh.
The one on the ground curses,
leans heavily on his gun
like a field hockey player getting
back on his feet. But he's
not a hockey player.
And that's when it starts.

# Suzanne Buffam

**Suzanne Buffam**'s (b. 1972) first collection of poetry, *Past Imperfect*, won the Gerald Lampert Memorial Award for Poetry and was named a Book of the Year by the *Globe and Mail*. Her second collection of poetry, *The Irrationalist*, was a finalist for the Griffin Poetry Prize. Most recently, she is the author of *A Pillow Book* (House of Anansi Press, 2016). Her work has appeared in international anthologies and publications, including *Poetry, jubilat, Denver Quarterly, Colorado Review, Books in Canada*, and *Breathing Fire: Canada's New Poets*. She lives in Chicago.

# Happiness Is Not the Only Happiness

My hair has grown well past my shoulders,
a feat I achieved by not cutting it.

Also this year I have learned something new
about daylight. It keeps us awake.

Likewise the moonlight, the searchlight,
the low blue glow on the dashboard

that carries each through her own private dark.
Rue is a sun-loving plant.

Tornadoes *want* us to chase them.
When summer finally arrives it arrives

in a rainstorm. Wind enters the spruce
and comes out wearing sparrows.

Some say water tastes best
from a bucket, some say a cupped palm.

## Ideal World

Nothing matters in an ideal world.
Not the stones you skip,
Not the fat birds overhead.

Run your fingers through the sand all day.
Lie still as a ship at the bottom of the sea.
Stick out your tongue

And taste the wrecked century
In a melting snowcone purchased for a peso.
All you taste is the taste of it.

Light plucks the coins from your eyes,
The heart spends its store
On a few everlastings

Jutting from cracks in the boardwalk.
Call it a kingdom nevertheless.
Watch the light black canopy

Lower from the west
Where a rust-stained tanker spins
A slow pirouette en route to oblivion

Via Sudan.
If you feel lonely
It's because you were borne this way.

If there are clouds here
They must be ideal clouds.
Clouds you can see through.

Suzanne Buffam

# If You See It What Is It You See

I didn't look at the fire.
I looked into it.

I saw a wall of books
Crash down and bury me

Centuries deep in red leather.
I saw a statue in a park

Shake dust from its fist
And a ship called *Everything*

Sink down on rusted wings.
Ten thousand triangles collapsed

Into a point
And the point was this.

I cannot tell you what I saw.
My catastrophe was sweet

And nothing like yours
Although we may sip

From the same
Broken cup all afternoon.

# First World Problems A to Z

Abstract art.
Blackout blinds.
Chemotherapy wigs.
Divorce court.
Existential philosophy.
Foreign rights.
Gap year blues.
Homebirth rallies.
Income tax.
Jet lag.
Kindergarteners carrying heavy wifi loads.
Lunch-truck fatigue.
Metacriticism.
Non-communicable, age-related cardio-pulmonary diseases.
Orthodontists.
Peckishness.
Quandariness.
Retro-modern décor ennui.
Second World problems.
Third World problems.
Under-enrolled inner-city charter schools.
Vanity publishing.
Weltshmertz.
Xfinity router outages.
Yoghurt packaging rage.
Zero money down.

# Mark Callanan

**Mark Callanan** (b. 1979) was born and raised in St. John's, Newfoundland. He is the author of two full-length collections of poetry and a chapbook. His most recent poetry collection, *Gift Horse* (Véhicule Press, 2011), was shortlisted for both the E.J. Pratt Poetry Book Award and the Winterset Award. He co-edited *The Breakwater Book of Contemporary Newfoundland Poetry* (Breakwater Books, 2013) and is one of the founding editors of the literary journal *Riddle Fence*. He lives in St. John's with his wife and four children.

## The Myth of Orpheus

And I came to in a room with a draft
that issued from beneath a swinging door,
my head plugged up like a sink stuffed
with months of shed hair,
shaving stubble, other things
that thought to disappear.

And the covers were bunched
at my waist like a marble effigy
of Christ newly sprung from the cross,
unveiling an inch of midriff,
my navel, which in the hospital light
looked like a wound from a hollow-point.

And the old man in a nearby bed
kept dying. The monitor would shriek
its air-raid warning and he would die
and come back. That was his trick.
He did it and did it. The slap-slap
of the nurses' soles was deliberate

applause. Then he left for good.
My wife said that when I was dead,
or during my death, she paced the garden
with my jacket on, cupping votive flames
to cigarettes. She killed each
match with a flick of her wrist,

then laid the burnt corpses to rest
in a packet scored with scratches
from matchstick heads that sought
to light the way, and did, and died.
Tendrils of smoke grew into the sky
as vines climbing from tomblike shade.

She stood, then, and helped me to my feet,
led me down the corridor
to find a cup of tea—past an orderly
who wheeled an assemblage
of bed, old woman, and IV—
not looking back to see if I was there.

## The Meaning of Life

It could be that this line drawn taut
between my fist and Bonnie's kite—
the nylon wings and plastic strut—
is closer than I'll come to revelation.
Or trust, I mean, in the sort of heaven
a feather's width between the fingertips
of god and Adam insinuates,
their faith enduring on a chapel ceiling.

I'm the kind of man whose mind
is often flocked with herring gulls
that dive for chicken skins in parking lots.
And yet, at times, I almost grasp
what's lost down on this lower plane:
the pull of unseen hands, a gentle tug.
Tangled string; me staring up.

# The Ship

I was in a bar between Duckworth and Water
on my way through a hooting mob
of clappers and stompers,
a swaying mass of drunk post-teens,
when this kid, bespectacled, barely
a sliver of bark off a birch rod,
pitched suddenly forward
as if standing on the deck
of a ship in heavy seas.
I caught him as he fell,
and ducking under an arm,
dragged him to the exit
like Simon towing Christ's
cross down the road.
Turns out he'd fallen earlier,
lost his footing in a puddle of beer
and struck the edge of a table.
Now, three drinks later, he was slipping
beneath whatever we take to be
our conscious lives. No matter.
I slung him on the steps across the way
and went to ring an ambulance,
the kid jerking like a dreaming dog
on the hot scent of rabbits;
frothing at the mouth now, rabid.
When I came back out,
good Samaritan, glad to be of help,
he was chatting up a pair of girls,
pants piss-stained.
I told him about the ambulance.
He said, *I don't know what's wrong*
*with me.* I don't know either.
What's wrong with any of us, I mean.

## Part of the Main

You might say that a clod washed away
diminishes the whole, the contours
of the land effaced by saintly
patience of the tide, which knows
that in time its tiny contributions
add up to subtract from the shore,
but this has all been said before,
and better, long ago. Carping on
about it like the bloody-minded sea
that drags its weight back and forth
across the beach stones—madwoman
at a washboard trying to scrub
away the stain of what she's done—
won't change the fact that it's easier
to turn your back on everyone.

Show me bloated bellies on the television,
dead children in their mothers' arms,
bomb blasts making burnt-on
crusts of people, and I will weep
a rainy season, clench my fists
until the nails leave lifeline sickles,
but otherwise do nothing.
I lack conviction. I am content
to have my outraged moment, then sink
into the comfort of an armchair
that won't protest when I protest
against the state of a continent
worn down by indifference.

Despite this slow erosion
of my sense of self
as a moral being, I am happy
paying for the services I'm given.
My rooms are lit electrically;
my rooms are heated.
And in the middle of a heated moment,
arguing with my wife over bills,
over money to pay for all the luxury,
I think: It's nice to have the luxury
of fighting over debts. So I find myself
indebted to people I have never met,
those murdered by my radio
while I drive the kids to school.
I kill the volume so they won't know
how much I owe the world,
or turn the dial to crashing waves
that wash away the dead.

# Chad Campbell

**Chad Campbell**'s (b. 1983) first collection of poetry *Laws & Locks* (Signal Editions, 2015) was shortlisted for the Gerald Lampert Memorial Award. His poems have appeared in *Brick Magazine*, *The Walrus*, and *Arc Poetry Magazine*, among others, and a chapbook of his recent work *Euphonia* was published in 2017 by Anstruther Press. Chad is a graduate of the Iowa Writers' Workshop and is currently undertaking his PhD at the University of Manchester.

# Iain Lachlan Campbell

The can command a room. The bevel-fisted
mayor of Sackville, the Renison Dean, sire
of four children. The wake up at six and read
the paper until his ears turned red and shook.
The recorder of the demise of his Canada,
the staunch, the solid, deliverer of grace at
dinner, the turkey carving, owlish eye-browed
thick-knuckled brooder, diabetic candy-stasher,
home-video Spanish-breast ogler, after dinner
own chest-napper, model railway builder,
false hip bearer. The devouree of cancer from
anus to eyeball. The caved-chest weeper,
holder of hands, composer of own elegy,
which I read, in part, shaking at the pulpit.

## Et In Arcadia Ego

Hard to make out a particular figure: the faces
pressed to the portholes, seeds stowed in oily
cloth, or a swaying lamp altering the hold.

The actual vessel & the metamorphic bridge of
a husband & wife: a ladder across the ocean, two
horses over land, the first stake as a crude house

coalesces from the forest. And we to thy service
build our homes on the acres, & as one generation
begins to stabilize the mirage with basswood & moss,

the *I must or else the wintry land will have them*
relaxes its grip on the family: barns tatter, rust
builds in the shed, field marking boulders slip

back asleep as trains bear the children away to
lift toil from the bones of the hand like a scythe
& try to balance it against a desk in their heads.

Some take podiums, some preach, one will invest in
machinery after a bullet whizzing through a tent turned
hair white as he stitched things back inside men.

Still others will undergo the loss of their minds
as if the same sheer will that seeded the stolen land
planted also a chaos that came boiling up like oil

or else they drifted through towns like glaciers, calved
in thin blue lunacy to commune with something terribly
wide. So our heads may have grown thick with others'

reflexes & to flinch under shadows in the ceiling might be
a house born burning in the child's mind. O distant country
perpetual, fields, fields of rye—even in Arcadia, there am I.

## The Fifth Season

Fifteen minutes in any direction is all
cornfields antlers and leaning
barns' definition of extinction,
porch collections of tins and paint
brushes writing down the most recent

myth of where our ghosts go
and whether they'll hold
here like the oldest teacher in town
uncertain if he emptied the vodka
before his cup filled with rain.

The town good fortune drove
through and kept on going, left
generations to sweep dust,
letters fallen from the theatre
marquee and the smell of diesel

persistent as the mottled
bark of the sycamores that cracked
before the brick face of the town
turned red and laid the rest
in the old river dreaming.

And you who left the town,
city after city while you sleep
curled like a question are
taken back on these walks
eyelids ghosted along the bare

lit streets lost looking for the reason
the shape of your leaving became
the shape of your seeing:
nameless as the fifth season
of the old river dreaming.

## Hear Ye

Come one come all to the Egyptian Hall.
Professor Faber waits behind curtains of
velvet, feet on the pedals to amaze you
with a voice built by human grace alone.
Stand & be dazzled by the opaque ribcage
of Euphonia—glimmer of the ghost
you want to know! Is she half human?
A spirit caged in the heart of the machine?
Watch a wizardry of fingers work *God
Save the Queen* from Indian rubber lips.
Seven years it took to haggle the vowel
E from wood. But if you stay when the last
aghast spectator leaves it'll only take
a second to receive the lobotomy of sheer
wonder, as Joseph works the bellow & keys
to wind a voice that sounds like the toes
of a skeleton sashaying over chestnuts.

# Dani Couture

**Dani Couture** (b. 1978) is the author of several collections of poetry and the novel *Algoma* (Invisible Publishing). From 2012-2016, she was the poetry and fiction editor at *THIS Magazine*. Couture's work has been nominated for the Trillium Book Award for Poetry, received an honour of distinction from the The Writers' Trust of Canada's Dayne Ogilvie Prize for Emerging LGBTQ Writers, and won the ReLit Award for Poetry. Her poems have appeared in publications in Canada, U.S., U.K., and several editions of *Best Canadian Poetry in English*.

## Union Station

I cannot love you all and I won't.
The shoulder knows the will of the heart.
The clam-soft give. The crack of the shell.

Talk in a low slow voice, wave your lunch bone arms.
The children with keys at collarbone are building fires
in the tunnels, forts at every junction.

Let them go. The way is littered with leftovers—
pale white stalks, tender volva. Pick one.

There are other ways home.

Brushed metal canines, the gate, will score
what you can afford to leave behind.

Impress me with your stones, your height.
The sweet dip of your neck.

All that you love,
keep high.

# Interview with the County Reporter

So many deaths that summer. Sometimes
I showed up and there was nothing more
than a stretch of empty road, a flipped car,
a body curled like a comma beneath a tarp.
Some passerby's offering of decency
before leaving. Last year's final dressing—
dried deer blood and hair still clinging
to flapping edges in hard heat, panting.
If it bleeds it leads, and our ditches
are brimming. The grid designed to bring us
together. Every four-way stop a lottery
of indecision, a place where front pages
meet obituaries. For a year of college midnights,
I made seat belts: the gentle shrug of poly
webbing, a stranger's hand to shoulder
the second before the crash. Either
it's something wrong with the design
or it's us. I've done my share of saving,
now tuning in to the scanner only nightly,
a redux of ten-codes: the newspaper
before it's written. A body propelled
through molared window.
We all have places to go.

# Salvage

*after the* Edwin H. Gott

You can tell a thousand-footer
by her straight back, hammer head
—a skyscraper toppled.
Too long for locks, what she's best at:
pushing taconite from Duluth to Gary,
the endless circuitry of ports.
Built from the centre of the earth up,
this ship is a piece of ceremonial armour,
a leviathan penny, a horseshoe
pinned to Great Lakes lucky until she's not.
Christened and kissed off
years before you were born,
she is an older sister, a summer cousin
who appears in only a quarter of your photos
and out of focus. She's your favourite
because you barely know her.
In smaller water, this ship could be
an island, a bridge, a territory.
She is a herd of 20,000 horses
trembling to shake off its load.
In her wake, lesser vessels are sent to scrap,
run aground, and peeled down to air, yet one day
it will cost less to wreck her than to keep her:
a final trip to Port Colborne. Breakers
will scrabble up her hard-rusted sides,
pull her down by torch and hand.
Her pieces soon held in the gut
of another ship downbound for better things.

# Contact

Cloud cover like a badly made bed, ruched in sections, rushed.
Whatevered for reasons of a lifetime of do-overs. Why bother
trying to change? The gathered duvet sometimes mimics you,
makes double. Dopples a decoy. An escape plan. The safety
of numbers and cover. When the wing dips, a hole in the sky
revealed. Until then, a man in the aisle seat. Calculations
to see if it's possible to slide through the fisheye window
if he touches your thigh again, your face. We like our planes
fashioned after ships. The illusion one could jump or be forced
off and possibly survive between the distance and everything
that wants to live how it's always lived. Without compromise.
When does knowing a person begin? Was it when he said
you look like his ex-wife? Hair naturally red, not like yours.
Fake. He can tell, but it's OK. What your children together
would look like. That if you had been born in Fayetteville,
he would've liked to have known you. Feels he does. Not
like the absent husband his mind weds you to. The one who
abandoned you to his company like a firing squad to its post
waiting for a reason to prove worth. The moment he asked
for vodka on the 53-minute flight from Charlotte to Wilmington
to bridge the gap between pre- and post-flight beers. Or how he lifted
his shirt to show you where his lungs had been punctured and once
collapsed, he said he'd briefly died and now is, briefly, alive.

# I Come Around with Appetite to Parties

An evening carousel of who died, which
winds ribboned down, and the difference
between something bruised or broken.

The treatment is the same. No, it's not
enough to say you were there, felt it snap,
or shuttered a photo. Instead, run a man's

finger along your chest and ask, *See?*
*Feel that. Right there? I think it's broken.*
Pain, like living, requires corroboration.

So he palms your left breast and pushes
until it gives. A sound. His opinion.
A hole dug and the declaration

of empty space as something new.
An inverse peak. He confirms what's already
inside you. Rib dispossessed of its hold,

the punchline out of sync. Meanwhile,
a mine shaft in South America collapses.
A deflation, though you are filling with things

that are not yours. What's broken rises
like loaves. You've been researching
these injuries, this news, for hours.

Tell me I'm right. That there's a difference
between a spout and funnel. A fracture
and separation. A plane that was cleared to fly

or wasn't. If the buk was stolen or given.
Birds kettle and people are kettled.
The kettle I forgot sings a high whistle.

The dead remain dead except we keep
finding new uses for them. A quartz
of quail's breast perched on worn gauntlet

can satisfy multiple interests.
How light the claw that only takes
what's offered when offered. We're told

every day is a rehearsal. Set the action.
Reach your end point. Reset. Remember
to look up and to the left. You're running

for your life. *The effects will be added
later, but we need your fear now.*
They gave me a blue and white dress,

sewed me in, but said I could keep
my own black shoes. Said, *If need be,
we'll cut you out at the end.*

# Kayla Czaga

**Kayla Czaga** (b. 1989) is the author of *For Your Safety Please Hold On* (Nightwood Editions, 2014), which won The Gerald Lampert Memorial Award and was nominated for the Governor General's Award and the Dorothy Livesay Poetry Prize, among others. In 2015, she published *Enemy of the People*, a chapbook of poems about Stalin, with Anstruther Press. Her poems have won *The Fiddlehead*'s Ralph Gustafson Poetry Prize, *The Malahat Review*'s Far Horizons Award and *Arc Poetry Magazine*'s Poem of the Year contest. She holds an MFA in Creative Writing from UBC, lives in East Vancouver, and works at "possibly the nerdiest bar in Canada," according to the National Post.

# Funny

On the bus today, a man looked like you with your teeth
removed, his lips a wild party on his face. Father, you
are not yet dead, though doctors keep removing bits
of you. *Soon you'll carry me around, a few floaters in a jar,*
you shout through the phone. That shouldn't be funny,
but is, the way it was funny you telling me to apologize
to objects I bruised myself on as a child—*Don't tell me
you hurt the cupboard door*. It stopped me from crying.
In this city where so many beggars look like you, I am
stitching what I know about you into poems, sewing you
together before you die, before I have to oblige you
by just dumping your body into the ocean. How do I say
you loved my mother through thirty years of sickness
alongside your love of pork'n'beans and Pilsner? To what
do I affix your Russian moustache? I know I will never fit
in the fishing lessons I failed, the gray days I wandered
away from you into the bushes. Father, I never told you—
I drank river water; I flipped over dead fish with a stick.

# Victoria Soto

In the poem I show to no one, a young teacher hides
her students from a gunman, lifts
them into cupboards—her hands smoothing

their hair, closing cupboard doors. Thousands of miles
away, snow falls into a small northern town
where I write, *Twenty children fell as snow. The light*

*turned less familiar as it reflected*
*off their bodies.* I've never been to Connecticut,
but I imagine a town hall filled with photo albums,

yellow roses, teddy bears, family members circling small
tables, retelling the story of twenty
short lives—*They woke, ate cereal, and a stranger walked*

*into their school with his hands full*
*of guns.* I stay awake all night, clicking through holes
in the internet, finding her photo, Victoria, thumb-sized

with dark hair, light eyes, clear skin. She stared
directly into the camera and then, how much later, hid
children in cupboards and turned

to the shooter to collect a violence the television
calls "random". It turns over in me, repeats as snow
repeats—on the radio, television, in the thin voices

of my neighbours—*when twenty children fell,*
*the world felt less familiar*—and falling again with each
retelling, the snow and the stranger,

the teacher who smoothed their hair.

Kayla Czaga

# That Great Burgundy-Upholstered Beacon of Dependability

Over dinner, my landlady laughs
about her day teaching rich Korean kids
the difference between a nightstand
and a one-night stand. Her son goes wild
for the bicycle pump. From his highchair,
he wails, erupting borscht. Refuses to sit
without its hard plastic denting his chin.
I don't get relationships. Once I got lace
panties in the mail from a friend who lives
in Winnipeg. He wrote, *I'm coming to visit
you at Christmas!* So I spent December
pretending to be busy, ice-skating until
my feet purpled, wondering how love
could transpire so oppositely between two
people. My mother once loved a grey van so
completely she sat in it for twenty minutes
every winter morning while it defrosted.
They listened to the radio together, to her
favourite tapes. The van went everywhere
with her, unlike my father who plays poker.
It lived for thirteen years in our driveway,
A great burgundy-upholstered beacon
of dependability, until its engine went.
I want to climb into you and strap myself in,
but that's not really love. Instead, we idle
in separate uncertainties, exhausting
reassurances. You thank my landlady
for dinner and roll away into a night
that imperfectly intersects my own, and I try
to stop imagining the ways we could fail
each other, and the people in rooms
everywhere who are continually failing
each other, and hope toward someday
having one nightstand with you, maybe two.

## Harvest Moon Lantern Festival

We got lost by the salmon-shaped lantern school
watching roe bulbs hatch into tadpole matches
and arrive in a field of lantern wheat transfixed
by how they lit candles so small. A lantern
thought bubble above your head says maybe
we could hold hands inside your jacket pocket.

A lantern reads, FOLLOW ME FOR MORE LANTERNS.
We follow the crowd following directions
on their lantern phones. Great horned owl lantern.
Lantern Hamlet lecturing his unlit skull. A bouquet
of carnations in lantern colours. A lantern your niece
made out of a soup can, three nails, and her feelings.

A lantern I just wrote. A woman plucks a harp
behind an illuminated nativity scene—which half
is the lantern? Two tweenage lanterns kissing.

An electric lantern shaped like nothing in itself
emits silhouettes of geese and sighs of mothers
disapproving recent piercings. Their lantern book
club has just uncorked another Malbec.

A man drizzling food colouring on a projector
is a sort of lonely man lantern growing cold
in a field of impatient children. Impatient
children in neon windbreakers are excellent
lanterns and continue burning past bedtime.

Lantern shaped like that ugly thing I said
at breakfast, quit looking at it. Lantern lime
as a hangover, crying into the garburator.
A lantern says, *it's your turn to do the dishes.*
Another says, *let's leave them 'til tomorrow.*

Historical lantern figures we've looked up
at since childhood. You photograph me between
Gertrude and a flying pig. Little boat who brought
my dad to Canada—float on that ocean of light
a while longer, ferrying souls to safer shores.

Click-bait lantern and us crowded around waiting
for kittens and life-hacks to load. It's too shiny
and aimed at us. I just want to carve a face
onto an orange vegetable with you, a big
crooked grin with three teeth, but I know
we'll leave it to rot on the stoop until February.

There's nothing like a lantern to make us guilty
for our many moods. There's nothing like a lantern.
Even in the hail it sits in its same face. Even
when I say, you're a real asshole, it glows.

*It's ok*, you say, *we're just lanterns waiting*
*for a volunteer's hands to place candles inside*
*us*—then the crowd might huddle in our light.
Though we're half-collapsed by the rain we'll look
more human for it, our faces clumsily papered—
*even though you're a real asshole, you'll glow.*

# Sadiqa de Meijer

**Sadiqa de Meijer** (b. 1977) was born in Amsterdam to parents of Dutch and Kenyan-Pakistani-Afghani origins, and has lived in Canada since the age of twelve. Her poetry has been published in a range of journals, including *The Malahat Review*, *CV2*, and *Poetry Magazine*, and was awarded the CBC Poetry Prize. Her first collection, *Leaving Howe Island*, was a finalist for the Pat Lowther Memorial Award and the Governor General's Literary Award.

Sadiqa de Meijer

# Pastorals in the Atrium

The tour has only started when
I'm ambushed by that flat-lined verdigris I'd know even
as a stumbling sleepwalker: *landschap*
with tin river, cleaver of sodden pastures —

marvelous for painters,
says the docent, was the enormity
of the sky, rarely cloudless, and she's already
turning to an Italian hillscape when I say wait! this is

my bloodstream, as my finger makes brief
unintended contact with the canvas,
and then my voice an ambulance
I tell her there should be a diagram
to indicate the grazing motion,
how the grinding molars of the Holsteins
make the river go —

or else, self-portrait
in the glassing-over eye
of a stickleback in a jam jar,
left too long in the sun —

but now the river is across the room because
the docent has ushered me toward an upholstered bench
and is murmuring, sit, sit, I have here from the staff-room
a coffee, here you are —

and I'm making the gesture for
no, those fields I ate and was made of
live in me, uncloseable
parentheses

## Introducing the Incredible Pseudomorph

There was a classmate's father who told me
I was special.

It was at a sleepover she was very popular not everyone
was invited.

Very, very special because of my parts white and dark together.

So.

Some squid, when there is trouble, release a phantom
in their own shape.

It has to do with mucus in the ink.

And everything with everything.

Sadiqa de Meijer

*sketch, pencil*

The light of television. Sunk in a blank
chair, glued to the Brandenburg Gate
or Rwanda. Just before ablutions
and half a sleeping pill. Late.

# Yes,

I said. The wind
lifted the word and blew it
through the birches into smaller yesses
that dispersed.

Hitched bicycle ride, my hands
on your waist,  soles skimming the road
in the bends.

What we wore will be one of those tellings
that even a latent, erasing disease
never steals. In tune like a robin and robin, a doorbell
and creak of the stairs.

Say love is the ship coming in.
Say the grave eyes of the birch trees
watched us go. How long

had we stood on the pier? Gulls squalled.
We'd outgrown what we packed.

## On Origins

Spoon, spoon

I, too, have a small version

I had one made
in the meticulous workshop
under my navel

They started with a fish,
then frog, then rabbit

And I asked them to stop at human

Like you, we are head over heels
when we look at each other

We go to sleep
concave, convex
in the room's particulate dark

Because I would know what to do
with a cranium slowly
gathering doubt

*Goodnight nobody, goodnight mush*

Mornings, we're sprawled
as if marooned

# Joe Denham

**Joe Denham** (b. 1975) is the author of a novel, *The Year of Broken Glass*, and three books of poetry. *Regeneration Machine* won the 2016 Canadian Authors Association Award for Poetry and was shortlisted for the 2016 Governor General's Literary Award for Poetry. He recently released his first album of songs, *Lost at Sea*.

Joe Denham

# From *Windstorm*

The boat burns in the windless night, its fire's
dark light threading in from the middle distance
over waveless water, black and slick
as tarmac after rain. The endless wick
of the city mauves the underbelly
of sky beyond, the boat burning slowly
northward on the flood, smoke rust and bruise-
black billowing off the flames.
                                           Forced to choose
I'd torch it down and take the money too.
One too many seasons in the secession
of seasons siphoning off the last life-
blood of a sea sick with eutrophication
till its death and the debt hone a knife
on the wind, course with self-scorn and blame –
the match struck and set, I'd swim from the flame.

## The Next Wave

Unseasonable snows blanket the windfalls
the branches, the timbers that once were
joist, beam and strapping here.
                              Sappho's
sweetapple, efflorescent in the unexpected
the unaccustomed white, perches bird-
like in song, as sunrays cloud-split; word
as though word were reborn, resurrected.

The weave – what's connected unequivocally
– unequivocally unraveling
                              on arctic outflows;
the disparity of what was given and what we chose.

And choose:
              I'll climb the ashen limbs
above this abandoned roofline as the west sky dims,
take that sweetness in as the autumn
                              and dusk transpose.

In the clear morning calm, in the quiet
fear, the first whisper of what blood-
light piercing grey cloud presages
in the charged air: the wire filament
surging spine, the sense: as the cold moon
siphons the tide, inside, beyond the cage
reason rages against receiving, this world.

I swear I collapsed on the float and unfurled
like a flag in the fast-rising wind. And lay,
bare as beach-washed bone, in the fray
we've sewn, torn, and re-sewn...
then rose, and turned my heart towards home:
your heart: from the gathering storm. Where
to begin, without ending, love? I love you. There.

# The Next Wave

My saw then silent the clearing reclaimed
the quiet it was as forest before I came,
engine in hand, orchard and house-site

in mind. Birdsong and a warm June rain
fell from and upon trees still standing
and for a time – a blue heron landing

atop the high fir over the iron pin –
I felt as I had as a child, before this
question of whether even to try is *ignis*

*fatuus*, when living and being in
the world simply was, not an idea
to be written of and discussed. Off the sea

a gust washed over broad maples, slanting rain,
and I set down to file the chain.

# Joe Denham

It is the world beyond weeping you walk through
its doors its wide fields with fading light

beneath the charred pines the delicate blue
veins, the diagnoses, the blinding white

machines. Having learnt, finally, to forgive?
This goddamn dissentious blood. This brain:

all of life's living just learning to live:
when water falling finally sounds it's no longer rain.

In time there will be pain and it will be
all I can do to rise and let the wind

through an open window, the distant sea
singing you through. Each night, each end

brings what binds us: our love, and fear.
It is enough, each day, to have been here.

# From *Regeneration Machine*

I pulled the truck over where the broom breaks
to the shore. There was little then stopping me
from not stopping, from letting the long box
follow me into the chuck. I rolled a smoke
and thought of my as-of-late-piss-poor luck
while smoke curled about the cab. The sea
spread out like a thick slab of slate, roiling
in the wind, as the cherry burnt like light
off a wire. Let's just say there is a fire.

And each thought is an injector ionizing the fuel,
the fuel igniting in the hole. This is as close
to the soul, or a vague sketch of the shadow of
its silhouette, as I'll come. I'm uncertain
what to believe of what does and does not occur
orbiting the sun. I let the diesel rumble and thrum,
each cylinder drumming its small compressive thunder
over the counterpoint of waves pounding the beach
as I huddled to the warmth whirring from the fan

and thought of your heart as it ran and ran and
for what? So it could break like a crash test
car crumpling against the brick wall of your brain,
its self-effacement, its pain? So you sent a bullet
straight into your skull. And that was that, wasn't it,
sorry friend? Sorry world, sorry witness, sorry
wind that sang through steel railings the sound of
bearings beginning to seize, their spinning straining,
as I climbed out into the rain and walked down

to be as close as I could to the gathering storm as
it heaved and sheared off the strait. It was getting late,
night gathering too, the islands' distant lights like a static
strand of stardust on the horizon. *As close as I can come,*
*which isn't very*, I was thinking, my thinking sinking
and sinking with the weight and violence of what
you once needed, my rejection cold as my chosen
occupation, the heavy block of that B-series Cummins
hanging like the garbage guts of my trade, our trade,

the last knot that bound us before you slid your finger
over that trigger and the afternoon unwound under
the shatter of the hammer. For years I could barely
stammer my own name, and then I was there,
in the leaden late light of that storm, choosing.
I awoke alone the next morning with the sun cold-
calling through the window. There was an angel
pruning her nails, backlit, on the sill. The backspin
of a bicycle's freewheel streamed sibilant through my street-

level window, the rider's voice singing over the click and whir.
The trick is to not do a double take. The trick is one
of light and of the mind and of wanting to believe we
aren't alone, in out hideous accumulation, without
the possibility of more than what we find when we look
upon the day finally, sleep rinsed from our eyes, and see.
That morning I heard the heavenly host of my own vestigial
hope lobbing lies over the waking border. I yearned to believe.

# Raoul Fernandes

**Raoul Fernandes** (b. 1978) lives and writes in Vancouver, with his wife and two sons. His first collection of poems, *Transmitter and Receiver* (Nightwood Editions, 2015) won the Dorothy Livesay Award and the Debut-litzer Award for Poetry in 2016 and was a finalist for the Gerald Lampert Memorial Award and the Canadian Authors Association Award for Poetry. He has been published in numerous literary journals and anthologies, including *The Best Canadian Poetry 2015*.

# By Way of Explanation

You have this thing you can only explain
by driving me out to the port at night
to watch the towering cranes moving containers
from ship to train. Or we go skipping stones
across the mirror of the lake, a ghost ship
in a bottle of blue Bombay gin by your side.
I have this thing I can only explain to you
by showing you a pile of computer hardware
chucked into the ravine. We hike down there
and blackberry vines grab our clothes as if to say,
*Stop, wait, I want to tell you something too.*
You have an old photograph you keep in your
bedside drawer. I have this song I learned
on my guitar. By way of clarification, you send
me a YouTube video of a tornado filmed up close
from a parked car. Or a live-stream from a public
camera whose view is obscured by red leaves.
I cut you a key to this room, this door.
There's this thing. A dictionary being consumed
by fire. The two of us standing in front of a Rothko
until time starts again. A mixtape that is primarily
about the clicks and hums between songs. What if
we walk there instead of driving? What if we just drive
without a destination? There's this thing I've always
wanted to talk about with someone. Now
with you here, with you listening, with all
the antennae raised, I no longer have to.

## The Goodnight Skirt

Permission to use that snowball
you've been keeping in the freezer
since 1998. For a poem? she asks.
What else? I say. I'll trade you, she says
for that thing your mom said
at the park. What was it?
"God, that mallard's being a real douchebag"?
Yes, that one. Deal, I say. Okay, how about
the Korean boy who walks past
our house late at night, singing
"Moon River"? Oh, you can use that, I say,
I wouldn't even know what
to do with it. But there is something else.
I've been wanting to write about
the black skirt we've been using to cover
the lovebird's cage. The goodnight skirt.
In exchange, I'll let you have
our drunken mailman, the tailless tabby,
and I'll throw in the broken grandfather clock
we found in the forest. One more, she says.
Last night, I say. The whole night.

She considers for a while, then,
Okay, that's fair. But I really had something going
with that lovebird. All right, I say, write it
anyway. If it's more beautiful than mine,
it's yours.

# Attachments

jamessmokingmarijuanathroughapotatopipe.jpg

lightsmearedghostsonthegreencouch.jpg

thekidwearingthepuffiestjacketeverandweallcallhimlittlelionwhichhe
seemstolike.jpg

marysshouldershighintheroom.jpg

jakeplayingwishyouwerehereonmyguitarforthethousandthtimeandall
ofusreallywanthimtostop.jpg

storytellinginthegreenhouse.jpg

thisiswhyevelynleft.jpg

sunsetpasthepowerlines.jpg

postsunsetcrowsflyingeastward.jpg

someoneborrowedmycameraandtookpicturesofmysiamesefighting
fish6of18.jpg

thisamazingspreadoffoodmycuporunnethoveretcetc.jpg

headphonesonadeerskull.jpg

damieninmidair.jpg

mydogcodysleepingonthebalconysurroundedbylonglegsgoingupforever.jpg

aliciagivesthislookthatalwaysmakesmewonderifthiswillbethelastpicture
ofher.jpg

colininaskirtsweepingbeerbottleglass.jpg

## Self Storage

*after Ali Blythe*

At parties I found myself drawn
to those who seemed most
like water. I love those nights

we were in slight disarray, showing
more ghost. *We'll probably forget
your name*, they said, *but tell it to us*

*anyway. Let's have it in the air.* And
isn't is strange that a poem has to
begin and end? As if it was a framed photograph

of a wave breaking and not simply
a wave breaking. My four-year-old son
intuitively understands the idea

of transformers. Once, as a plane,
he lay down on his stomach, arms apart
so passengers could enter the doors

on the side of his ribs. I don't know why
we'd have such trouble with this. Did we
read too many books upside-down

and with anger? Could we not do the extra
second of homework when a stranger
enters the room? There's a diner along

this highway where with infinite coffee
and infinite time we could solve this.
Transform ourselves into prisms

or creeping vines or a stack of poems.
Better poems, I think. Though we're bound
to fail for hundreds of years, first.

Passing the SELF STORAGE building
with its quiet climate-controlled rooms
makes me smile. The *Smile You're*

*On Camera!* sign in the dollar store
doesn't. I can clip the labels from
the inside collar of my shirt but it just

itches more. Paint over my storefront
awnings, but the original text ghosts
through. When I borrow someone's pen

my handwriting changes—somewhere
halfway between mine and theirs.
But a few pages in, it's mostly just mine.

Almost. Not entirely. By the end
of the long night we've built adapters
upon adapters so that all our devices,

no matter from what place or time,
can talk to each other. By then
we're so exhausted, our code frayed,

the floor a tripping hazard of tangled
wires. Still though, right? Dawn's light
surfaces like homework solving

itself. Our ghosts massaging their
equations. I'm sunk into the couch,
thirsty as hell, dreaming a river

that flows right through the room.
A river I know I can drink from
because it's moving, clear.

# Autumn Getty

**Autumn Getty** (b. 1972) is the trans female author of two books of poetry, *Reconciliation* (Nighwood Editions, 2003) and *Repose* (Nightwood Editions, 2008). She has also published two chapbooks, *A Gentle Shaking* (Junction Books, 2000) and *Lyric and Elegy* (Biblioasis, 2006). All these works are published under her former name, Adam Getty. She is the recipient of the Gerald Lampert Memorial Award (2004), the Hamilton and Area Arts Council Award for Poetry (2004), and the Hamilton Arts Award for Writing (2012). She has been shortlisted for the Trillium Award for Poetry (2005) and the Premier's Award for Excellence in the Arts, Emerging Artist (2010). She currently lives in Hamilton, Ontario. She attended the University of Toronto but left without taking a degree.

Autumn Getty

# **R e p o s e**

I've taken rest on a boulder in this clearing
to finish thinking on it while the quiet's
still hovering around me. I'm like a spring
someone is flattening until it lies
uncoiling on the ground, the tension light

now pressure's been removed. I wanted rest
but not this closure: things were piling up
and I was full of them, and being pressed
to take on more. I couldn't interrupt
the constant flow of work because I'd slept

poorly or the load was heavy: weren't
we all carrying too much? The noise
is what I miss—the shackle line's chain
like glass bottles clinking after toil,
the scald tank's clang amidst the seething boil

was the sound of railway cars as couplings claimed
them. Always the drone of the main line,
the slowly turning wheel and its rusted chain
often mistaken for the hum in my mind.
All I hear now is the cicada's whine

and in its pauses a distant rush of cars
climbing the hill to Ancaster recedes,
its mechanical dying like a far tide
rolling from the solid land. Maybe
the spring's uncoiling is different than mine

and I'm a red-breasted robin that's never
left the latticework of limbs and leaves
for the deepening dark sky and now is severed
by consuming fire and a thick corrupting sleeve
of bitter smoke, smoked out as though a beetle

had emerged from dark wood thrown on a rising fire.

# Pender and Hamilton

I'm seen sometimes along old Frank's peninsula
road, there to tend my flocks, sheep
and swine both. I love the little roads, though;
cement or dirt, it doesn't matter. Signs,
private, don't come in. I would, unknown,
if only the poor things knew I lived openly
in dark and light alike. I like them thinking
I am kept out, for when am I more near
than when beneath the cool sheltering branch
they bend forelegs beneath their pliant necks
and rest their restless eyes? No matter
if even I am shut out; I love to turn
and look upon the placid valley road
that climbs and falls though never breaking—
the hills when distant seem to swell, until
I can't believe I live within their shadow.
All is nameless here. One side, grass flat
to exposed stone, pale, chipped by the vast
native wind or rain, the sharp rolling cry
of lightning's strike, the creeping moss
a swell of life to cover stone like people
upon the earth. To the north the land
falling away: a buckling fence, the snake's
hole that runs beneath, flimsy wall
for the rotting shack tilted toward sea, and,
further on, the painted ships upon
a painted ocean. Be still, now, and look
upon your work: you laid islands like stones
and pulled their peaks toward the sky, a quiet
line of sentries that keep the Malaspina
waters in ordered calm. The mist like incense
ascending, flung to earth, ascending again,
a gentle repetition under the white-capped
spirit that watches and approves all. Wait,
Pender, let your reveries cease;

for one unknown is climbing your hill—
he'll think you mad. I've heard another wanders
here now, some old toolmaker, a scent
of coolant marking him, or varsol, if
the day is ending. Let me try him.
    Hello, fellow walker, stranger, friend:
pleasant to rest a moment, catch one's breath
after so steep a hill. The sun is dimming,
and casts the slopes and growth, the water-glimmer
and roads in stark relief, the best moment
of the day. Tell me, stranger, of the road
you've travelled, of your land and work.

    A stranger in a strange land: all my life
this saying teased a yearning within me,
a hot enticement, like the lure of false
women – the place I settled in was once
so full of blood but now is cramped and stiff
from lack of movement. Every day the people
continue, squirrelling the work away:
in Stoney Creek the headless hogs will hang,
eviscerated, bloodless, half a year.
I lie, as we all do, to tell the truth—
after a day the animal is cut
to pieces: boned for hams, whiz-knifed
for tenderloin, for good and tasty meat
to sit uneaten. It's hard to think one's work
useless, desolate, to put an end
to effort now the need is past. Ontario's
distant shore is an emblem of its people:
the beach's curve became a block of steel,
a chart, division into lines, assembly
of patterns – what use is freedom now?
The people want to build, to can, to smelt
and slaughter, to count the wheels and spigots
rolling off the line, to pile them high.
All the senseless work: to stand a dozen

meandering hours cap-spinning shampoo
or dumping glass for juice, or scooping sugar
into churning vats for syrup, lifting rail
and cutting it so trains could switch their tracks,
all glassy-eyed tedium till I walked
away from every job, what was it all for?
To lightly kick a skid one idle minute,
waiting, rare reprieve, while merriment
is borne upon the wind like drifting snow
to pierce my ear? Unknown, and spread like jam,
like a last attempt to save the spoiled fruit,
to sweeten others' mouths? Unfair:
you caught me thinking, and I spoke too soon.
My words were all complaint, and empty, artless.

     You, artless, a craftsman? Surely not,
to think our poverty wealth. Mountain soil
brings forth seed-bearing fir and pine
cradled marsh-weed, moss upon the stone,
indeed all life requires to creep about—
do not confuse the verdant hill with moneyed
ease. Look closer at that down-slope shack,
that bit of shredded fence that closes it in,
unkept: but for the spreading green and view
of sheltered waters they are poor as any,
if poor is what you seek. Not poor, I think,
but living capably. It's wealth that's strange.
I think it unnatural.

          Unnatural? The word
is nothing, spoken only to lift our image
beyond its worth. We heft a hammer
and call ourselves tool-users, as if the ant
could carry nothing to the building site,
the mounds like cities, or the chimpanzee
used no stick to fish in trees for food.
The ones that know: the world is what we know,

our place in it.

Uncommon, then.

Wealth,
uncommon? No: this hill presents a view
of harbour, hills and mountain, a mottled pleasure
for the eye too vast, imprecise. Near Warnock
I stood upon a smaller hill, near a lot
with little silver domes and flowers set
in rows of pots – a deer considered the earth
in silent rumination, still as a thinker
with fist in mouth. Her stillness not of thought
or comfort: in the field of rich grass, fear,
a sudden unity with sense. With twinning
hooves she clomped away – as we all must.
False to speak of reason, instinct: I watched
intently as a spider spun its web,
pulling and extending spindle-legs
with thought, precision, tireless effort, caught
in strangeness, as if watching women knit
or men tie up rigging, intricate lives.
An hour it mesmerized me with its work,
then rested in complexity – mistake,
for now its spindles radiate like fossil
remains upon my book, life crushed from it
for fear of poison. Its labour desolate.
I looked and thought, what difference is dying
there, what odd thing passes? No odd thing:
a body, organ of nerve, the world-finger
sounding sorrow with this chord, or anger
with that sharp, a man like me. An end to it—
spider, deer, my mind will tend to add
import to stillness, reverie. I meant
the deer is heir to ease and plenty, even
the spider with its fishing net cast in air
knows little travail.

# Jason Guriel

**Jason Guriel** (b. 1978) is the recipient of the Frederick Bock Prize and the Editors Prize for Reviewing—both from *Poetry* magazine. He is the author of several collections of poetry, including *Satisfying Clicking Sound* (Signal, 2014) and *Pure Product* (Signal, 2009), and a book of criticism, *The Pigheaded Soul: Essays and Reviews on Poetry and Culture* (Porcupine's Quill, 2013). His writing has appeared in *Slate, The Atlantic, ELLE, The Walrus, The New Republic,* and other magazines. He lives in Toronto.

## Less

—cooked by crooked
math—is more
than enough.
For example, the rough
patch on the roof
of the mouth we tongue—
a light fixture, chandelier
of texture—is so much
more than mere
canker. And when
fingering the clasp
on Father's snuffbox,
his fine initials
grate against our
fingerprints' grain
like an engraved last gasp.
Less, being more, makes
of the tectonic plates
of molehills
a mountain ridge
the way the stark plain
of the *White Album*'s sleeve
raises the Beatles' embossed logo
to the level of topography—
the way tiny things
can't help being, next
to nothing, something—
the unanticipated mole
that makes a one night stand's
upturned ass, the last leaf out
on a limb, the little
going a long way.

Jason Guriel

# Empty Nests in Leafless Trees

embarrass the bare limbs
that still bear them,
especially at sunset
when leafless trees become
their silhouettes
and empty nests
tend to stand out
like mashed clots
in a fine mesh of capillaries
or ink blots
in failed calligraphy—
those spots
where nibs have bled
into the fibre.
Actually, I lied.
Empty nests in leafless trees
aren't similes
or metaphors
or, for that matter,
even matter.
They're black holes
that sucked their birds
inside.

## My Father's Stamps

Like a gallery wall without a theme
or a wall of windows
that won't make up its mind
and vacillates on the vistas
it gives way to,
the typical page of paper my father
stuck his stamps on
is drywall in a dream:
eight and a half by eleven inches
of plaster whose portals
(perforated squares)
look upon a world
of incongruous parts—an Eiffel Tower here,
two wrestlers knotted there,
a biplane crop-dusting this corner,
some Queen ennobling that—
panels in a comic
book without cause
and effect. But because
he can no longer say the names
of this stuff his stamps frame—
because of the stroke—
my father can only point
to and take a tally
of these windows he long ago
decided would go
together, even though they opened
onto different kinds of light
and weather. So I turn
the pages. I point out stamps
I know to be his favorites.
But I want the well-meaning
nurse (who stops to feign an interest,
leaning over the stamps

and speaking in the baby-talk
that seems to be an old man's birthright)
to stop and look again:
this is the work of one
of the great surrealists.

## John Hancock's John Hancock

makes wind
the way it whirls
about and blows
the neighboring names
of other signatories
away. The point
of it is not
the John or Jane
Doe it names;
the point's the quill
in motion as if
still stuck
and aquiver in
goose skin.
The trick to writing
well isn't up
the sleeve. It is
the sleeve
that fluffs up
the flourish,
that blooms around
the stunted stamens
of the fingers
and distracts us
from our grasping
for the sun
or the uncertain
scratching
of the stylus.

# Leah Horlick

**Leah Horlick** (b. 1988) was born as a settler on Treaty Six Cree Territory in Saskatoon, Saskatchewan. Her first collection of poetry, *Riot Lung* (Thistledown Press, 2012), was shortlisted for a 2013 ReLit Award and a Saskatchewan Book Award. Her second collection, *For Your Own Good* (Caitlin Press, 2015), was named a 2016 Stonewall Honour Book by the American Library Association. She is a past winner of the Dayne Ogilvie Prize for LGBT Emerging Writers. Leah currently lives on Unceded Coast Salish Territories in Vancouver.

## Little Voice

That morning in the motel
    where your best friend lived,
new snow outside, at least in the memory

and the stranger—he was eighteen,
    you were alone, she was downstairs
at the pop machine or something

while you watched the snow, the nest
    of beached antlers in the yard
behind the pine trees and then he was there, too

in the room, telling you about
    a guitar, or something useless
and you thought

*empty room*, you thought *quiet house*,
    you were a very smart girl and you felt
the footstep he took one step closer behind you

at the window, and from the rising star
    of your gut you heard it, like twin
drops of water—you have to leave the room

*Right. Now.* And quietly, and you did.
    That was *smart*. You were a *smart
girl*, and you did not tell anyone

not when they found out he was
    in her room at night, not
when they sent him away, not

until you were a grown woman, and what
    you wouldn't give
for that little voice again, now.

# Amygdala

It names you gazelle and it calls
*lion.* Stomach churn and lung-hover,
it reroutes the canal of your breath
to quadriceps, large muscle clusters,
the limbs you hold closer

when the flowers arrive it says *fire
alarm.* When the new lover or victim
sits in the front row it says *brimstone*
and it says *yes* to tequila and *yes*
to shaking, always, knees and hands,
under the arm of another woman it will name
*safety*, it says *go home with her*, you must

go home, avoid the tall grass and public
places, the darkened lot, the stampede
of small crowds and also solitude, go home,

the amygdala says this
is the savannah and you,
a gazelle.

## Anniversary

It has taken five years and fifteen hundred
    kilometres to get away, and closer

to the mountains. I can see them—
    every day, like I always wanted. Near,

and distant. Every day I can ask people
    not to touch me—

on the bus, on the beach, or in my new kitchen.
    Or, I could ask them to—

which, lately, is harder. How can it still
    feel so soon? She has never been

near this new body of mine—
    short-haired, tattooed, very strong

and very, very fast, now. I carry a chunk of rose
    quartz the size of my thumb for safety.

I have sworn to myself a life of people
    who know when to stop. I promised—

and spent my first night in the new apartment drawing
    circles in salt and rain, whispering

to my old self, come here. *I built this*
    *for you. I promised.*

## There Must Be A Name For This

How to feel like how you imagined the city? A blur of light steps out of a cab. Stem of a glass in a ring on a wet table. Slink, slink. Would it have been better if you had moved into that little beehive level with the SkyTrain, whoosh all day, glow all night, little hexagram. One stool, one door, two windows at an angle with the tracks, tracks, track. Two windows! Rattle rattle goodnight all day. You imagined glass and water, heels and click, the film of alcohol across everything, city city. Little dots of light, little swipes. A secret: Vancouver is actually a series of small caves, mould like a dust of sugar powder, did you know? Saturday night aesthetic: the Chevron station for yachts in Coal Harbour, hovered out in the water, glossy black, little ring, orange light. How long did it take me to realize the white-hot squares at the top of downtown are penthouses? How long did it take me to realize those very regular fireworks are private planes? Why can't I have, why can't I have, why can't I? What if we just kept living together, what if I just tried harder, what if I *had* moved to Toronto? All the women in this city say *I love you*, they say *centered*, we say *seawall*, we go home and murmur *Toronto Toronto Seattle Toronto* in our sleep. You don't understand. I have an obligation to a girl in a barn, to a girl in a car, to a girl in the forest; she says Get Me Out Of Here, she says My Own Apartment. Is it possible to be dissociated not from me but the city. Like here I am arms and legs, here I am oh *New York*.

# Liz Howard

**Liz Howard**'s (b. 1985) *Infinite Citizen of the Shaking Tent* won the 2016 Griffin Poetry Prize, the first time the prize has been awarded to a debut collection. It was also a finalist for the 2015 Governor General's Award for Poetry and was named a *Globe and Mail* Top 100 book. Howard received an Honours Bachelor of Science with High Distinction from the University of Toronto, and an MFA in Creative Writing through the University of Guelph. She is of mixed European and Anishinaabe descent. Born and raised on Treaty 9 territory in northern Ontario, she now lives in Toronto and assists with research on the aging brain.

## Terra Nova, Terraformed

Spent shale, thigh haptic fisher, roe, river
delta of sleep-inducing peptides abet our tent
in a deep time course, in Venus retrograde

we coalesced into the Cartesian floral pattern
of heritage where I hunt along a creek as
you pack bits of bone away within a system

of conservation the site was discovered
during construction of a new venous
highway for stars birthing themselves

out of pyroclastic dust and telepathy
in the time zone of some desperate hour
when all our exits are terraformed

Sons and daughters of the liberal arts
all my life has spurned a desire for more than
a power line of injured transistors

fetal alcohol syndrome, oil drums sunk
to the bottom of every lake, the aurora borealis
an overdose along the magnetized pole

what we are offered in lieu of a soul
another paper cut of lambent plasma
thickening the wound bed of release:

O creek, bleeding hills, census inveterate
let me sleep five more minutes just five
minutes more before we default on

eternity

# Look Book

Over there on the green
lawn under a sick pine
is the body of the bird
his plumage blue when
I go to look at him and
wonder if he's dead but
his chest sort of heaves
so I bend down closer
look how the breast
of the bird splits open
and a fist of maggots
spills out on the grass
a necklace of sticky
pearls in peristalsis ribbed
and shining in the July
light invertebrates that
form an anecdote before
I go back into our clapboard
house to look at the Sears
catalogue and dream
I am a girl posed into
happiness look at me
here now in this new
dress I've bought with my
own money at age twenty
in the city when the cops
question me I flash my
passport thinking of
lichen inching down
a branch of a tree over
the town river when I was
small and somewhere my
birth father is drunk and
homeless, half-mad when
the cops ask for his name
he'll say, *December*

# Euro—Anishinaabekwe—Noli Turbare

Beauty is my irreparable and today I became geometric.
A faux linear figure that distills a skip trace of First principles.
In a whiteout of Atlantic snow banging stars into the femoral
vein of Euclid while rows of lavender circuits, all porous,
surrounded me. I genuflected before the hospital parking

of my father's jaundice, for I am a good daughter of the colony.
The colony which begot the immortal heart of the markets.
Resource nursed all young bucks of the florets, a liquidity
I should service or else receive a lesser dessert. With my smudge
cleanse at the ready I find myself dispensing with the usual

future haunt of stability; a survival signaling my relationship
to time, or I'm out of it, entirely. Chanting hell as hair veils
my face as if this is a Western. Come polygon and I circumvent
the disaster, *do not disturb my circles*. Holy I went, holy
all around my head, the holy I am went careening down

the back stairs of this low-rise rental. Striated by the pinnacle
light of this city that has my blood pooled purple at the center
of its gravity. You can scan the ground from overhead for death
pits. I read this on the internet when I was dehydrated, lonely,
and afraid. Office plants all broad-leafed repositories

for cognition's patent heart. I've gone and been abominable.
A column extended from the top of my head into heaven.
At the edges of my system an Anishinabek or Indo-European
projection of words my nerves could translate into the crawl
space of animal magnetism. White pine verticals send us up

as a stomach pumped by filial love. Oh, inconsequent curb
of my street I refuse to kneel, this day like any other, a cousin
charged with trafficking. Still waiting to be ordained, I make
mask of our features that are retreating. Plush pockets of rust
about another falsehood of water, a creek that pleats. I've gone

and got a blister. That summer a black bear's muzzle was coated
in shellac from the aerosol can she bit through on my mother's
porch. A half-century after my grandmother's mother said,
don't ever shoot a black bear, they are my people. So I continue
to speak more than this mortuary sunrise where I am only just alive.

Boozhoo, today is over.

## A Wake

Your eyes open the night's slow static at a loss
to explain this place you've returned to from above;
cedar along a broken shore, twisting in a wake of fog.

I've lived in rooms with others, of no place and no mind
trying to bind a self inside the contagion of words while
your eyes open the night's slow static. At a loss

to understand all that I cannot say, as if you came
upon the infinite simply by thinking and it was
a shore of broken cedar twisting in a wake of fog.

If I moan from an animal throat it is in hope you
will return to me what I lost learning to speak.
Your eyes open the night's slow static at a loss

to ever know the true terminus of doubt, the limits of skin.
As long as you hold me I am doubled from without and within:
a wake of fog unbroken, a shore of twisted cedar.

I will press myself into potential, into your breath,
and maybe what was lost will return in sleep once I see
your eyes open into the night's slow static, at a loss.
Broken on a shore of cedar. We twist in a wake of fog.

# Stevie Howell

**Stevie Howell** (b. 1977) is an Irish-Canadian writer. A first collection of poetry, *Sharps*, was a finalist for the Gerald Lampert Memorial Award. Stevie's poetry has appeared in Canadian publications, including *Hazlitt*, *Geist*, and *Maisonneuve*; in U.S. publications, including *BOAAT*, *Prelude*, and *The Cossack Review*; and overseas in *The Rialto*, *The Moth*, and *Southword*. Their critical writing has been published in the *The Globe and Mail*, *Ploughshares*, and *The Rumpus*. Stevie Howell is the poetry editor at *THIS Magazine*, and an MFA candidate at NYU. Stevie's second book of poetry, released spring 2018, is called *I left nothing inside on purpose*.

# Rip Torn

Almosted into marble by medusa-eyed hoi polloi
The Queen's stone jowls, eraillure of crow's feet,
are freshly quarried—fifty years late,
her face is lithic flaked into a lustrous, toothy smile,

as electricity excites mercury vapour, she is lightboxed,
backlit, mounted every few paces in the chambers
of the London tube. Her cumulonimbus-hued
bust, the size of Easter Island moai,

is shit-grinning over diamonds, on exhibit for the great
unwashed to grub up and drool over. Jewels encased in
UV-proof acrylic vitrines, whettingly
argon sandwiched, cannot be made stonier by our

countryside-bred, dazed un-blink. We share our sheep's
hypoxic shrug at the Lorenz curve of the earth.
We leap magpie-footed, shriek obsidian
disbelief tidings, fervent for useless, shiny things.

The Janus of the Jubilee and Olympics has her visage
pinned to the bricks and loitering in tunnels; a tattered
flag to the proclaimed, uncharted
country of herself billows above the footbridge—

the gammon display is reminiscent of Styrofoam castles,
glue and sand. Mickey Mouse and the Magical Kingdom, Iraq
under Saddam. But my companion says, No,
she looks like an albino Grinch. She looks like Rip Torn

in a Swarovski choker and cotton candy wig.

# Crunches

So one Hallowe'en I was a Playboy bunny
and my boyfriend—ex-boyfriend—was Hugh Hefner
I wore this, like, totally slutty thing—

> I'm going to be a Victoria's Secret angel
> which is neat because my name is Victoria?
> But I can't tell anyone, I don't want them stealing it
> I'm gonna wear a thong—

Ya, over some lace hot pants—

> I have hot pants but I gotta add the lace, and tights—

How about no tights? Just baby oil your legs, it'll look sick—

> I gotta hit the gym—

It's, like, totally crunch time
those two weeks before Hallowe'en.
Do 1,200 calories a day, lots of water,
60 minutes of cardio, and crunches—

> Crunches is, like, your middle name—

# A Girl's Will

So frequent, I think of that bleak town,
landlocked, parched, miles from the Blackville brook;
countless times I have gone walked up and down
dusty streets with my hunchback mum
while the townsfolk snuck their look.
And a verse from an old Longfellow poem,
learned by rote, haunted me as I shook:
'A girl's will is a leaf's will.
And the thoughts of youth are close, close thoughts.'

I can trace the dusty line still, can recall
passing the farmhouses boys burned for thrills,
the chalk parched acreage we hand tilled
in flour-sack skirts, where we hammered the mound
of our pet rabbit. The land seemed to crest uphill,
to cliff off at the edge of the world. I kept
one hand on the porch at dusk, in the light of the sill:
'A girl's will is a leaf's will.
And the thoughts of youth are trembling, trembling thoughts.'

In our finest, whipping through minus, we rode
through winter into town, hitched up the dogsled.
We paid last season's debt and ran up the tally
for another hibernation. In a hand-hewn, not-plumb box
kids lined up on a lumpy straw bed, clothes
in parallel perked on the stove. The wind hyperventilated,
and the words swirled around my head:
'A girl's will is a leaf's will.
And the thoughts of youth are close, close thoughts.'

Our food strung in a sack, its mouth
wedged under a bank rock in the years before refrigeration.
After summer, the river was diced into ice blocks
for the barns. What wasn't wanted preserved also relied upon
the elements—the drop and dissolution—mewing kittens
in a weighted, cinched pillowcase, tossed in. Those years
I feigned deafness to their lesson:
'A girl's will is a leaf's will.
And the thoughts of youth are trembling, trembling thoughts.'

The words flame out, a winter's breath.
A dandelions' geodesic seed-dome scattered.
After supper we played with a knotted pig's bladder,
a homemade balloon. The stolen hen we snuck to
the woods, for a secret teenage *boulier*.
Whoever else knew is lost, or dead
now and memories matter only to myself.
'A girl's will is a leaf's will.
And the thoughts of youth are close, close thoughts.'

A candle is cold comfort to a woman who had
to drop palmed tools because the sun was setting.
Endless labour—the opposite of today's
prolonged births and stagnation. Over my mother's
crocheted tablecloth, torn web of mending,
you skip the prayers, strike a match, and dim the lights
for atmosphere—that's everything; the century's been upended.
'A girl's will is a leaf's will.
And the thoughts of youth are trembling, trembling thoughts.'

## Rain Pool

Let's ride on mountain
bike to the haunted house. Empty-bellied
ppl drawn

to shadows.
Cicadas climb toward concert pitch.
Asphalt fumes,

skinned knees,
fresh cut grass. A love for anything gutted.
A melted toilet

hangs in strings.
Bubblegum. Porno mags strewn in rubble,
a post-hoc shrine.

Gum whets
appetites. So do boys. So does the sun.
Where'd they go

the family
who fled here, united in chorus as cicadas.
A superfamily.

Pop quiz:
What's worse—sunstroke or hunger?
A curfew

or latch-key?
If freedom is chaos, chaos is love.
It's love, then.

It's cool. We swim
in the haunted, rain-filled kidney pool.
Coitus is

so funny
such a sex-ed word for it. Gobs of leaves
ghosts grabbing

our ankles
are reeds in a northern lake. No, were in
a reef

somewhere equatorial.
Schools of surgeonfish brushing by
our coral limbs

are as harmless as
they are beautiful. You never asked
to be born.

Neither did
the oblong orbit of my mother.
Water trembles

the moon.
What we've found is as beautiful as
it is harmless.

# Amanda Jernigan

**Amanda Jernigan** (b. 1978) grew up in rural Ontario and as an adult has lived in Ontario and Atlantic Canada, working as an editor, scholar, and teacher. She is the author of three books of poems (most recently *Years, Months, and Days*) and two chapbooks (most recently *The Temple*), plus the monograph *Living in the Orchard: The Poetry of Peter Sanger*. She is an essayist as well as a poet, and has written for music and for the stage. With her husband, the artist John Haney, she publishes occasional books and broadsides under the imprint Daubers Press.

# Aubade

The time, if time it was, would ripen
in its own sweet time. One thought of dawn.
One felt that things were shaping up,
somehow, that it was getting on.

Day broke. Upon the waters broke
in waves on waves unbreaking and
night fell, unveiling in its wake
one perfect whitened rib of land.

I slept, and while I slept I dreamed,
a breaking wave, a flowering tree,
and all of one accord I seemed.
I woke, and you divided me.

## Catch

My father was holding a ball in the shape
of the sun. The sun,
he said, at four point five
billion years of age, is in its prime:
with more or less an equal span ahead
before, its hydrogen depleted,
it begins to slough its shells and eat
its children, a red
giant. By which time
you, my son, and I will be long gone, and all we love.
And then he tossed the ball to me. I didn't mean
to catch it but my hands reached up.

# Lullaby

My little lack-of-light, my swaddled soul,
December baby. Hush, for it is dark,
and will grow darker still. We must embark
directly. Bring an orange as the toll
for Charon: he will be our gondolier.
Upon the shore, the season pans for light,
and solstice fish, their eyes gone milky white,
come bearing riches for the dying year:
solstitial kingdom. It is yours, the mime
of branches and the drift of snow. With shaking
hands, Persephone, the winter's wife,
will tender you a gift. Born in a time
of darkness, you will learn the trick of making.
You shall make your consolation all your life.

## Beasts

*In my kind world the dead were out of range*
*And I could not forgive the sad or strange*
*In beast or man....*
            —Richard Wilbur, "The Pardon"


He told me of the Cape-Town walkup where
he lived till he was eight; the years spent there,
he claims, his best,

although he'd range his wooden beasts, some nights,
along the windowsill to watch the fights
outside. At last,

presumably, his folks were reconciled
to moving—this no place to raise a child—
and made to flee.

The family came to Canada, where not
much happens for a lion or an ocelot
or boy to see—

where I grew up, and entertained myself
with fairy tales from which I'd struck the wolf,
though now, I've found,

I summon wolf and lion, woman, Lord
knows what, and bid that wooden horde
to laager round.

# Aisha Sasha John

**Aisha Sasha John** (b. 1980) is a poet, dancer and choreographer. Her solo performance *the aisha of is* premiered at the Whitney Museum in June 2017, and will close the MAI's 2017/2018 season. Aisha is the author of *I have to live.* (McClelland & Stewart, 2017), *The Shining Material* (BookThug, 2011), and *THOU* (BookThug, 2014)—finalist for both the Trillium and ReLit Poetry Awards. In addition to her solo work, she choreographed, performed and curated as a member of the performance collective WIVES (2015–2017). Her video work and text art have been exhibited in galleries (Doris McCarthy, Oakville Galleries) and was commissioned by Art Metropole as part of *Let's understand what it means to be here (together)*, a public art performance residency she designed and led. Aisha has an MFA in Creative Writing from the University of Guelph, and a BA in African Studies and Semiotics from the University of Toronto. She lives in Toronto.

## Self-Portrait Cemetery

There was no precedent
just a headache, despair, three
cans of Asahi plastic-bagged and
there they were:
most punched into the earth like
square stud earrings,
the rest pushed out, erect,
fake flowers at their base the most
colourful pubic hair.
One grave said Lagos, Nigeria so I stood
by it clasping the beer with the full stretch
of my hand.

I was the only live body around.

# They moved my friends

into the chicken coop.
And where are the chickens?

I wished the lambs a pasture the size of the donkeys'.
And I wished for the donkeys—
I wished something very large for the donkeys.

I am a donkey.

There was ginger ale, coke zero,
and Mexican beer
on the small cart of the small donkey.

The large and
heavy head of a
donkey
covered in several burlap sacks.

## This is what I will say.

I physically got what I wanted.

Experiencing my return to a prior interest (unnecessary comma)
I realize how uninteresting
of a shape a
spiral is:

your blessed life
lying against your stupid life.

Attending an event in which you can
guarantee admiration
and then suffering that admiration ignobly.
Almost ignoring it.
As if it is the natural physical constant circumstance of your life
unlike
the longing for it physically.

Aisha Sasha John

# **Something softens me**

Softens my desire
Something helps me breathe
Something spills out my pores as light
Something
Is like hope blanketing me
Something bleeds as me
Bleach
On a stain
On a blouse
In the day
Fading at the sink.
I scratch my head to flakes.
I return to
My reading.

The first knowledge is of our ignorance.
Hi.

What's seeable and not
I join
For those to whom I'm betrothed.

I am the bride of your listening.

# Evan Jones

**Evan Jones** (b. 1973) was born and raised in Weston, Ontario. His first collection of poems, *Nothing Fell Today But Rain* (2003), was a finalist for the Governor General's Literary Award for Poetry. In 2005, he moved to Manchester, UK, where he has lived since, completing a Ph.D. in English and Creative Writing at the University of Manchester in 2009. He is co-editor of the anthology, *Modern Canadian Poets* (Carcanet, 2010). His second collection, *Paralogues* (Carcanet), was published in 2012. He is Lecturer in English at the University of Bolton.

Evan Jones

# The Horn Gate

It is not the sea you hear. Not one of the five rivers of Hades nor rain against the house you grew up in. Over the past four thousand years, this gate has become more popular than its partner. I wandered two weeks to get here, book in hand. On arriving, I leaned back, pressed the pages flat against my forehead, and began to cry. This is not what you hear either.

## Nausicaa

She remembers only her dreaming. Refashions herself in the morning as if sleep has removed a piece of her, changed and replaced it before she woke. I, too, am at her knees, have been for some time now, but not as part of the dream. She cannot see me lying waterlogged on the sand in front of her; steps on my hand and walks by. It doesn't matter what I am. There is a certain pleasure in that.

# Anteros

Imagine the breath inside you belonged to another. This may take some adjustment. Inhale. Every day, do you empty or refill your lungs? Niobe's children, their chests pierced by arrows resembling beams of morning and evening light, understood that no cherub killed them. Exhale. I worry that you might misunderstand.

# Self-Portrait with Argus
# the Hundred-Eyed

Many-eyer, many-eyer, many heroes
    are dull, children of Dutch
millionaires, sons of Prussian princes,
    who bear the names
of champagnes known the world over;
    and through our fifty-one
telescopes we glimpse the moon,
    the stars, and Venus,
when the clouds clear long enough,
    all unimportant but present,
a manageable version of the evenings
    wasted herding and flocking,
while you could take a city single-handed,
    you could go to the dogs,
or otherwise turn up your toes—sing
    here we are again!—
the moon presiding over the chestnut tree
    and then beyond it,
the acacia losing a leaf to the wind:
    all this behind you now.

Evan Jones

# God in Paris, 1945

Since the world ended He had been living
there, coming and going along the length
of the trembling Champs Élysées. Free
of the stars and prayer, His work tragically

out of fashion, the old city had seemed
as good a place to wander as any
and so, being wandering itself,
and swarming solitude, He paced along

the cobbled streets like a child lost in peat moss.
The Germans were gone, Céline with them,
and Jean Lumière singing 'Faisons Notre
Bonheur Nous-Mêmes' in cafés stung His ears.

'Either the universe is infinite
or I am,' He remarked to passersby,
'Either the universe is finite or
I am. Or I'm not. Or I'd better be.'

If you reached out to touch His hand, even
accidentally, you will remember Him.
For your hand is stone while your eyes and hair
are the wind that opens and shuts my book,

an ocean and sixty years away from
His room in the Hôtel du Marais, third
arrondissement, an unknowable land.
O rise wind, take my scattered pages

to vast and empty Paris. Either God lies
in a bed of earth alongside all
of history's dead or He doesn't. Or He'd
better. Whatever way wind, don't let up.

# Sonnet L'Abbé

**Sonnet L'Abbé** (b. 1973), Ph.D., is the author of *A Strange Relief* and *Killarnoe*, and was the 2014 guest editor of the *Best Canadian Poetry in English*. Her chapbook, *Anima Canadensis* (Junction Books, 2016) won the 2017 bpNichol Chapbook Award. She has work in *Best American Experimental Writing 2016*, and in her next collection, *Sonnet's Shakespeare*, L'Abbé "writes over" all 154 of Shakespeare's sonnets. She lives on Vancouver Island and is a professor of Creative Writing and English at Vancouver Island University.

# Killarnoe

Killarnoe is a place I invented right
now. I just built it from my head. I started
with a letter k and set down the letters
that spilled out. What does that say when k-i-l-l

first sprouts? Something repressed, or
an instinct, that when allowed a moment's
free reign, opens to its own mind
and speaks bluntly? But see how I persisted

past the first impulse to slash at the page's
clean white throat, and instead adorned it
with a pretty vowel, gently drawing out the ells
to sulk the k down into a rumbled,

grudging argument against the mind's knee-
jerk proposal, the oh opening to compromise,
and a silent e watching without judgement.
Killarnoe, I decide, is the land

of our ancient people.

## Repetition

The sound of the drum
means the teller's gonna come.
  *The teller's gonna come.*
  *The teller's gonna come.*

The sound of the drum
means the teller's gonna come.
  *The teller's gonna come.*
  *The teller's gonna come.*

Hear the hollow sound
from a skin above a round
and a hand slapping circles
at the sky

Feel the way your feet
on the ground will mark the beat
and how the tapping trip
can get you high

You hear my peace propaganda?
  *this is my peace propaganda*
Come hear my peace propaganda
  *this is my peace propaganda*

Close your eyes and feel
how the rhythm helps to heal
the cacophony of crap
inside your head

And be aware of he
who says repeat after me
Follow only if you won't be
blindly led

## Sonnet L'Abbé

This is my peace propaganda
    *I don't know but I been told*
Come hear my peace propaganda
    *people buy what they are sold*

# Ah

An open moment,
a prolonging
of notice
without reaction, a downward
fountain of data, filling.

Unclosing, throat's
wholeness, wide,
to swallow
the thrall of all of it:
full bulge of gulp
held—

nothing undulating, no
void vacuum
pursuing a present cud
through
a human tunnel.

Sustained hum,
sustenance
pouring, not pulsing.

Rinse without erosion,
flush without the closed
push of peristalsis.

Clarity
not needing blur
to know itself.

# Brain Stem

Strong neck the channel through which your roots become branches. Strong neck the trunk through which your impulses flow, tides of perception and reaction. You are a battery of cells, positive of material, anti-positive of nervous potential. You, a dyad of bunches of waving branches and bundled branches, of bunches of searching roots and rooting roots. The spine of your decision-making: a flexible tension between head and heart. The moving tree grows in more dimensions than knowledge: in its reach, yes, in its span, but also, if it is lucky, in its rootedness, in its density, in the neck's rough skin thickened to injury, that lifts above its heart a head of power—ever spring-fond, ever fall-wise—a tender, leafy power to love light.

# CXXVIII

How often when we dreamed, Dad, was the dream house mentioned? You imagined a rustic plot, exposed beams, a huge studio out back. A piece of land for clay and fire's meeting. Studio-pottery-as-return-to-the-land: Steele did it at Nanoose Bay; Laffin and Ngan established wood kiln workshops on Hornby; a hippie team with potter Lari Robson sought and found their craftsman work hideouts above Booth Bay. Those West Coasters wet their fingers in salt water while you, Northern Ontario kid, lugged your kin to Calgary, to cast with Askey and Ungstad, to throw wetware with Gord Robertson at Ceramic Arts. Your communal enclave of potters was a different whack at modernist *mingei*, commercialism and craft confounded, a business-minded Orientalist folk movement. Did you make those jars, or could they be Katie Ohe's? The unknown craftsman ideal might work for humble village potters of Japan, but in commercial markets, your mark is your aesthetic take on Leach's brand, named and circulated. The inward, forceful touch of your hand, its weighted, skilled pressure, left impressions—your pots' forms like performances of workmanship, each an ethos of harmony, of function (how well does that handmade pitcher pour?) balancing individual expression. Stoneware napkin rings, teapots with cane handles, wood-fired soup bowls, decanter sets, mugs by the hundreds, bottles, jugs: your shapings of extracted land, in folk tradition borrowed by avant-gardists and Black Mountain ceramicists, were work. You lived the philosophy, threw as though art worlds rewarded character, fine galleries' patronage would heighten our state and situation, and sweat equity in handcraft would build that house. That dream, utopian fabrication, forged me. I chose inkjet and paper as rough materials; in workshops, practiced forms. By touch my fingers now know how to translate, to make, my rawness into a thing, presentable, wedged out of capitalist making. I'm living the dream on the Island, in Harewood, in the middle of nowhere. Blessed, I guess, to chase such singular surviving. Meanwhile, hobbyist potters step into your space just to sit with authentic mastery. Japan jacked Korean skills; did Shoji Hamada live appropriately? Lari died in two thousand twelve. Robin Hopper's garden lives on. For this poem, an internet search of your early work found just two things. A casserole on Calgary Craigslist. And a late mid-century decanter. This vintage guy in Lantzville, whose teak lamps decorate my bedroom, has it. He balked at a discount, even though I said I was your kid.

# Ben Ladouceur

**Ben Ladouceur** (b. 1987) is the author of nine chapbooks and one full-length poetry collection, *Otter* (Coach House Books), which was selected as a best book of 2015 by the *National Post*, nominated for a 2016 Lambda Literary Award, and awarded the 2016 Gerald Lampert Memorial Award. In 2016, he completed a three-month residency at the Al Purdy A-Frame in Ameliasburgh, Ontario. He has lived in West Yorkshire, East Sussex, and Toronto, and currently lives in Ottawa, his hometown. His second book of poetry will be published in 2019, also through Coach House Books.

# Armadillo

My lover spent his summer in the south,
carving armadillos from their husks. It was, to hear him
say it, an experience—the term people save

for the places they hate. He spent June in the sunroom
with a pitcher of sweet tea and a picture of me.
By August, just the tea, watching hicks

suck cigarettes through long, aristocratic
sticks, papaya seeds stuck between their burnt
sienna teeth. Everything was burnt there. My lover

carved years off his life with the very same knife
the armadillos learned to fear. *Where are they*
*now,* I asked him as snowfall took care

of the candles I'd lit. *The not-quite-rodents, the not-quite-reptiles,*
*not-quite-right gatecrashers of the ark?*
*How does their nudity suit them? Do they sigh*

*all cool, how we sighed last year, when we threw our anoraks*
*off and found we had that chalet to ourselves?*
*If we were ever blameless, it was then. I held your locks*

*in a Chinese bun as you went south indeed,*
*throwing, upon my balls, your tongue, how sea urchins*
*throw their stomachs upon the coral reefs they eat.*

At which point my lover raised his knife
to my hairline, scalped me masterfully and poured,
into my open brain, a tea so cold and sweet.

Ben Ladouceur

# I Am in Love with Your Brother

Richie made me promise not to relate any stories of
embarrassment or crime, but, Richie, on
this, the evening of your nuptials, I must tell them about
our long day in Truro. I just must. The fallacy then
was a dark twin of tonight's fallacy, we
and the dogs—who are thought to be clairvoyant
on these matters—anticipated storms
that never came, and here we are now, beneath
a tarpaulin, on an evening they reported
would be clear and ideal for regattas.

As Truro woke, as Truro's rodents spat their
morning songs, Richie came across my notebook, open
to its core, and spotted my little admission:
*I am in love with your brother.*
The first line, I insisted, of a song I'd been arranging
to be played on the Wurlitzer, though now I
come clean, Richie, while your soul is at its smoothest
and most forgiving, I did love him, the crimson acne
flecked across his neck, he was like a man
a guillotine had made an attempt at.

We rolled that whole notebook into joints, didn't we,
Richie, then drove into the boonies to shove ammo
into rifles folk left above their porch doors.
That summer, your brother's motorboat
slipped into the Irish Sea, his mannequin body
demolished, and I'll bet he is here now, and is
glad, I am sure of this. Caroline, Richie
is one hell of a guy. You would do best to keep
his body firmly in yours, how seas contain boats,
for he is only stories to me now.

## The Masturbating Flowers

Ignore me—I am frail today.
If I tell you to stop
walking, keep walking. If I ask

for a piece of your nectarine,
or press your palm
against my chest, where the ribs sink

most, where your come, months
ago, would collect and grow cold,
keep walking. All around us,

library books used to wilt and expire,
and if we were outside,
the masturbating flowers

would bite their filthy lips.
Sitting in the narrow shadow
of an infantile willow,

with a paperback, and a highlighter
to mark the words
we wanted in our lives forever.

The penultimate embrace, abbreviated
by such factors as the arrival
of the streetcar and the heterosexual gaze.

The ultimate, unabbreviated: a decadence
of unclean teeth. I've since begun flossing.
There's blood sometimes so oral

has been taken off the table.
A raw gum is a head wound, like any
other, a door a blight loves the sight of.

It gets men all choleric, though.
In the yellow light, with their yellow feet,
they push my body away.

## Vulgaris

I was on my bicycle the week of the lilacs.
The blossoms were descending and the birds were down to fuck.
I was not their target demo but I forgot.
So see-through and clean was the song the males made for the females.

Dandelions congregated via wind and beaks and generations.
They will go far and yellow the whole world with their clones.
I will die and they will yellow and amalgamate my bones.
The thought of it all gives a human an important headache.

Humans sing too but not all their songs end with the genitals showing.
If I pedal too fast my bike sings a song about brokenness.
The lyrics are: you will die.
The lyrics are: maybe soon for I am old and unsafe.

I ignore this song even though my bike loves me and sings it for my benefit.
I pedal go pedal go pedal until my brain forgets that it is not inside a bird.

# Jeff Latosik

**Jeff Latosik** (b. 1980) is the author of the collections *Tiny, Frantic, Stronger* (Insomniac Press) and *Safely Home Pacific Western* (Goose Lane Editions) as well as the chapbook *Helium Ear* (Anstruther Press). In 2018, his third collection, *Dreampad*, was published by McClelland and Stewart. His work has been included in the *Best Canadian Poetry in English* anthology in 2015 and 2016 and recently been nominated for a gold metal at the National Magazine awards. His work has appeared in *The Walrus, Maisonneuve, The Puritan*, and *The Malahat Review*. He lives in Toronto.

## The Piñata

They came to strike the piñata.
The piñata hung from a crane
and swayed, its swollen gut
of newspaper and paste.
They listened as the piñata creaked,
a dock in choppy waters.
They began to shout themselves to the brink.
And standing there, watching the piñata,
it seemed almost possible
to forget the search that had continued
since Christmas, was it this one
or the one before?
Parks, rivers, cupboards, drawers,
the bent light beneath their decks—
what had they found?
And standing there, the piñata swaying,
they were gathered and ready
with hammers, bats, knives and chains
to smash and tear until the piñata's shanks
could be nipped by dogs.
Though when the first seam split,
some resorted to doubling over
and pawing the grass.
While others continued taking swings,
the halved ones moved with new insistence,
their hands sweeping over the ground
like visible winds.

Jeff Latosik

## Song for the Field Behind Mississauga Valley Public School

The field that stretched beyond
goalposts. The field that redrew
lines in us.

Like the field in a glove save.
A high-five. The field in a radio hit,
its raised seating.

Or, the field in waiting. The field in hunger.
The field in a fifth beer, a wrong turn,
the field in the little scar
on your neighbour's forehead.

The field in every abandoned thing
we found in that field. In every bent putter.
Torn jacket. Set of keys.
The field in forgetting. In debt.

# The Internet

I first heard about it in a Burger King.
Its aims seemed as elusive as the stock ticker
or why some people stayed in marriages.
The future was flying cars, phone screens, and Minidisc.
I bused tables with a cloth that mucked the laminate sheen
and, just that Spring, an annular eclipse ringed the sky
like we were suddenly looking down a cabled conduit.

Then, as if an indigenous strain moving beyond a range map,
people started *getting it*, birdsong calling up from basements,
the pink noise, hiss, and crackle of a connection made.
And somebody already had some pictures: the body,
pixelated, bare, with the feeling you were overseeing it,
moving along the conveyer belt of banner ads.
Days went by like they were being dragged into a bin.

Somewhere, fibers tethered us to a warehouse or a factory,
but for then the feed seemed as ephemeral as a thought.
The search bar like a mail slot you could lift
just enough to see inside somebody else's space.
It wasn't a place, but you could go there.
At night, blinds down, but windows open, flags of light
were quietly raised from main floors up into our rooms.

## Foley Artist

This is the sound I was trying to make:
in the film in the film, they're shooting a big-budget prequel to *Jaws*,
but the rubber shark heads are being eaten by a real-life shark.
*The sound of the rubber pieces being chewed—*
not easy, but I'd done harder and worse.
Which makes me think. I knew a boy named Kevin
when I was too young to know the difference
between rubber and real, though rubber is real,
and Kevin knew a place to hide in the valley so good
that no one ever found him though he kept appearing
startling people in their sliding doors. He was locked in the glass
as if he'd done something so sinister his punishment
needed flair to amuse the ones who'd been wronged.
Once, though, someone snapped a photo
and swore it was Kevin there, watching—we all knew
it was bunk, the person knew too, but then we started
talking about it: *do you remember that time*
*I stuck a pin in his waterbed for no reason really*
*or the time he got dressed up as his mother but not in her clothes?*
We retrieved the old albums, unpacked the taped boxes,
found the one botched life-sized drawing
he'd done of himself and completed it
together as a neighbourhood, a district, a city,
practically a nation at this point, and then a sort of galaxy
expanding outward at a speed so great that when Kevin
walked out of the picture with a boom
it almost wasn't a surprise, so fast were we moving...
But Kevin was back, and he shook our hands,
revealed the crevice he'd made in the dirt
and told everyone sorry for pulling this stunt.
And then he lived his long life. He married,
had children, difficult years, divorced, rebuilt—
and double back to the start again on this slight tilt:
in the film in the film they don't need to add any sounds
to the mix because the shark that swims in and chews up
all our likenesses is already perfectly captured.

# Mind

Having one means you've got to be
at least two about most things.
Take how easily we forget
the liver, spleen, and heart aligned
in a way the mind seems to want to fly above
and disassociate itself from finally

in some thinner sphere where knowing
has the air of everything that's seen as right,
for now. And buoyant there, it wants
to have so much figured, so much
deftly navigated as if *that* made one kind
of elevation truer than another.

Hold that against the morning after,
the accumulation of the body's clatter
which stutters language. And damaged
matter under MRI makes a case
for lessened responsibility.
The mind might still insist it's skyward

and all's going well, not landing anything
on water. Where was I in all of this,
however? In one way, somewhere
on the ground, making smoke semaphore
from the Urals out across the Bowels
trying to guide the mind down with a gut feeling.

# Canisia Lubrin

**Canisia Lubrin** (b. 1984) is the author of *Voodoo Hypothesis* (Buckrider Books, 2017) and *augur* (Gap Riot Press, 2017). She is consulting editor at Wolsak & Wynn and an editor at *Humber Literary Review*. Lubrin also serves as advisor to Open Book and teaches college English. She is the 2017-2018 poet-in-residence with Poetry in Voice.

## Voodoo Hypothesis

Before sight, we imagine
that while they go out in search
of God
we stay in and become god,
become: Curiosity,
whose soul is a nuclear battery
because she'll pulverize Martian rock
and test for organic molecules
in her lab within a lab within
a lab. She doesn't need to know our fears
so far too grand for ontology, reckoning.

Did you not land with your rocket behind
you, hope beyond hope on the tip of your rope
with the kindness of antigravity slowing you down,
you, before me, metal and earthen. But I am here to
confirm or deny, the millions of small
things that seven minutes of success were hinged upon
when I was little more than idea and research,
in the hypnotic gestures of flame and Bunsen burner,
and into parachute
no one foresaw, the bag of rags at the end
of the tunnel—all memory now,
this Paraclete.

Where else is a pocket
of air more deadly than the atomic bomb?
Would this only happen on Earth?
Has Mars run out of tolerance for the minutiae
of air pockets, fingerprints and worry?
Aggregates of metal, Curiosity
and her clues to calm our fears for what's coming.
Mars and her epic storms, her gargantuan
volcanoes have long ceased their trembling,

her crazy flooded planes, frozen and in cinema.
Martian life now earth and revelation's phases:
Earth problem, not Mars problem.

But why
should I unravel over all this remembering?
          Great thing about landing
          is that I've arrived

at your service, at your sand, at your valley
and unsentimental magma.
Before me screams planes like Mojave Desert, Waikiki, Nagasaki,
nothing too strange to keep Curiosity off course.
Even though the Viking missions found no conclusive pulse
and we declared you dead, O Mars,
never mind that we named your heights and depths
from orbit. And from your spheres of minerals
where oceans once roared—we've learned little
of your lenience for empire.

Forgive us what Spirit uncovered in the silica of your ancient hot springs.

Ah, yes, we've come back home.
Phoenix told us we inherited the numberless
stories of your hydraulic pathologies
but I am Curiosity. If I kill the bitch right,
she'll take us deeper and convince us to send earthlings
to set up Earth colonies on your deserts. They won't ever
come back, but that's not so bad when we trade in
the grander scheme.
As though the colonials, the Tribe Traders
and all the pharaonic masquerades of gone times
were not fair threat. That we won't know the depth
of our homeward seas
is nothing when
the sun's still got our backs.

# The Next Wave

And while waters still vaporize before us
Curiosity will keep on until the organic secrets
of that Martian puzzle become as household to us
as carbon. Oxygen wasn't the only disaster to befall Earth,
to bless her with life.

Apollo drilled on the moon and got stuck
and the harder we've drilled down here
the more we've loosened our screws.
Perhaps there'll be no one left to give
a damn about the death of our privates

unless we prove ourselves enigmas,
the alien we think we know is the alien we only dream
up starting from the bottom
of the Curious.

We wake and die through
the crowns and thorns and craned chapters,
we move too quick for understanding.
Still, through the decades we predict,
Curiosity confirms the cold-slain dust.

Then come her conches blown
in the hard-won postcards travelling
on space dust faster than a bullet
to say:

*hey,*
*I'm here. I safe. Wish you were here.*
*See Gale Crater, Mount Sharp, just as you've said.*
*Come bask with me in the wonders of a Martian. Good afternoon,*
*you of flowering faith. Set sail for home,*
*because we will all wear the consequences of this choice.*
*And you never should have said*
*goodbye.*

## Keepers of Paradise

This is a hand that intends to do its maker harm.
This is the clock turned back five hundred years.
       The river that runs from Eden mouth
       to rare unsweetened mouth.

I've logged the sour dawns of all
my quiet into this body,
its crisis of fleeing nowhere when nowhere is home.

And reborn half-bled in our nighttime
diverging their sullen brethren, their patterns of vapour,
rain, shadows on goat-eaten planes
in the Morse events of smallest things
in my new metropolis away.

I am a simple child, then, a tilled site of history.
Call me isobar. Distraction in place of earth.
Call me tropical depression

      where I regale to the world its problem of beaten pines,
pleading rivers returning thorns to their abducted bush.
I'd offer the wound night shuts behind my eyes—

But enough. Hear Morne D'or divinize her song.
      Give these coon keepers of paradise a liminal eavesdrop.
Hear ghostly algorithms translate these nights to bloom.

# The Mongrel

*There was no name for us in our mother's oratory.*
　　　　—Saint-John Perse

√

Still unravelling from ghosting stars,
she moves us, light-formed, cue,
of Mongrel, also a corpse, but of steel,
curved, down earth's scrubbed sands,
on a single gust of wind,
and her body through a doorway,
she shrinks hundredfold,
to size of Earth: moments ago, forgotten,
now dreamt Mongrel: a fur city, no more
archival than ancient than still warm and
she'd done nothing except bawl *the lost,*
*are enough!* The science, inexact like birth
is Mother, Mongrel alive in the street-chained light—

≅

If from above, the Mongrel's Creole maps
mathless, a late-life scar that carts its wounded
head on the surface of a jaundiced stream, she—feral
with remembrance, her black-rock heart must hide
pressure-cooked islands, stormed space where
Einstein's quadrate bones scurry to mount Nèg maron.
　　　　Slave-hand revolts at the green mouth of Hades:
　　　　how Mongrel rites wrap fur against a Native
　　　　is address to Caliban, the animal that knew it had been
brutalized by men. But fine. By now, the seas are vague,
and even the exploded Carina spares us, wanderlust
and relative need for lightspeed, systems and fall-off—

≠

There is blood, seldom ache, where the avail-
able light reaches down past levels of dog,
cow's grass, tribe, pitch and burn, the wild
brutality loves us this side of the name, while
only misted, our ears stretch to still the Mongreled
air landing, broken, invented again as *history*
          in the rusted coils of coffee shops, inked
Mongrel skins, whose only escape is one cosmic
blue carbuncle. What is the right way to sway
the Black bruising self, elegant as a question
mark can curve into harp and vein and matter,
dark with blows like from God, cannibal and castoff—


≥

The Mongrel was still breaking, offing,
in a pale blue nutshell of monk's milk and tar
when life exposed the carapace of her skull.
Bit, where ancestors drew their roots up
those walls of knotted blood, on a throne
that names a million years into entering an illusion
          of singed bamboo, then ships
come and night comes and stays and soon
these generations miss their gills, scales
and talons, still dug into old valleys, still
lulled by disappearing suns, by broke hours
of bone branding flesh, held dark through
immortal dark, a gleam of that riverine name—

≤

Inside the wounded name, she gathers like dust
down the corduroy route, the Mongrel
heart in her hand—once part of a waist-high
Earth, then life upward started with the trees and
untroubled by the termites, still one hundred
million years off and withered on the brow of chance.
Together, they disappear to plot with the cliffs
   from which will protrude pavement
and aperture, time: a Mongrel's walk to the place of these pines.
Collapse, then, into leather boot and this smoked hunger and re-enter
the story: that Nova Scotia beach aglow with Mongrel flame—

∞

Now if she knew to sit, downed by the blunt breath
of doubt, would she have troubled the Mongrel
with music and milk and names and trenches,
those miles so deep? What else reveals us, a species
of amnesiacs, cut off from the trembling that tore—
our continents apart? And with so much unknowing
like this view, like rising smoke reveals the Eden
continent, preserved in the blind spot of a pictured
confession: this grief, a story with swords and bite, sun
whose silence holds the invisible pulls of distant worlds, wars
unhinged from the shoulder blades of gods. The Mongrel's
orienting grace is still its tail, showing up for things to come,
signalling that our knowledge of the Mongrel is only fragmentary—

# Nyla Matuk

**Nyla Matuk** (b. 1967) is the author of two books of poetry: *Sumptuary Laws* (2012), and *Stranger* (2016). She has been nominated for the Gerald Lampert Memorial Award and the Walrus Poetry Prize, has received a Yaddo fellowship and grants from the Ontario Arts Council and the Whiting Foundation. In 2018 she was the Mordecai Richler Writer-in-Residence at McGill. Her poems have appeared in magazines and anthologies in Canada, the U.S. and the U.K. such as *The New Yorker, Poetry, PN Review, The Manchester Review, The Walrus, The Best Canadian Poetry in English,* and the *New Poetries VI* anthology (2015).

## Don Draper

Moths feather your far gazebo
like young sailors on first leave.
You know something, and keep reminding me

of my own needs. You see an audience
of blooming heads and sugared bank notes,
and act accordingly. The swallows see it at five o'clock,

a Wolfman's tragedy.
They hang themselves upside down,
handsome sienna prizes in the semaphore of bats.

Swayed by a summer night, I swing out
to your silk pocket square standing at attention,
a bird about-face. You're the dark dew on the green grass of home.

Nyla Matuk

# Poseurs

The walking stick insect was a late childhood horror,
ugly as an umbrella's disrobing.
Moths, with brown wings the prize of
Asian fan-makers, pestered it like paparazzi.

That Peruvian variety, a race almost entirely female,
would come down from the Morello cherry long after sunset;
after the plums turned the humid blue they want to be,
after trees sighed and inhaled the nearby jasmine, blooming
them nightly to dream-lives as smooth-complected date palms
for some caliph's odalisque
or the low-stress Oregonian monkey puzzles,
a species whose softly-prickled, rounded shoehorn limbs
propose new kinds of orgasm.

Walking stick insects
were squibs from the natural world,
little stand-up comics
fashioned after mutineered twigs. Given half a chance,
the poseurs would neither walk, nor meander,
perambulate, or otherwise imitate
Wordsworth or Nietzsche. Like the wives of 17th century
men of garden science, they loitered and lolled
between vivarium and cabinet of curiosity,
dividing their time between joy and sloth.

# I Declared My Ethnicity

About the boxing kangaroo, there can be no doubt.
With gloves, on a stage, they made a man of it
and outperformed those wondrous catalogues:
all the colours, all the birds, all the seashells,
all the words in the novel *Clarissa*.
Tense developments during some performances. As characters
fly up and down the stairwell, gowns flutter and fall.
Add details to set a scene: a filigreed banister,
a large potted palm; the thrilling notes coming out of
that rare breed of grand piano.

My origin story involves merchants plying
between ports of call across the Mediterranean,
one more arousing than the next. I looked into a mirror
and saw the Portuguese girl. I declared
my ethnicity on my latest biographical note, only
to reap what I so forthrightly did sow.
Do I look artificial in this mask, I ask.
You'd mention it in the 1970s, and they'd say terrorist.
You'd mention it in the 1980s, and they'd say terrorist.
You'd mention it any old time and they'd assume

a portion of white where there was none. You mentioned it in 2014
and they said, 'but are you Muslim?' Whether by logic
or by fantasy. So instead, I decided to watch miniature TV
and mind the shop: small Bruno Gerussi, small Aretha Franklin;
small Al Waxman, small Flip Wilson. Knowing all this,
it was as if orders of world magnitude were getting
down to fighting weight, becoming poems of the cult of personality:
my kitchen is your kitchen, type of thing;
but enough about me, what do you think of me, type of thing.
How about giving those gardenias sighing in a nearby
vase an opportunity to speak up? Then again, they're so white,
they aren't all that troubled. But there is comfort in flowers.

We'll always have flowers, tragedies, timelines, mainstream
media, and those large, eavesdropping porch moths.
We'll have a heaven for flowers, almost as important
as their ever-dying scents. And in what remains, in the dry-down,
I will say, what a beautiful falsetto.

# Stranger

*on the* Ethan-Allen Express *near Cold Spring, N.Y.*

A wail in a minor key along the Hudson Valley shore.
This train calls to familiars. A pond of swans
under a red maple consults in the folds
of its bishopric. I thought of an evening two Junes ago.
The first of the group of schoolgirls on the sidewalk
started to run. The others started to run behind her
in their party dresses, all yelling, "Don't run! Don't run!"
laughing and looking like they were having
the time of their lives. I noticed one girl
near the back of the group, laughing and yelling
after them, a bit taller, darker, swept up in it
for no other reason than itself. Lost now too,
sitting in 14B in pashmina and dark glasses,
I might as well be the Smyrna merchant.
I've never been good at small talk;
besides which, we'll be in New York in about an hour.
Later that night, I remembered the way she laughed
as she ran, and in the morning, her face
was the first thing I saw when I woke. It seems now
she'd shown me what had come to me once
and was now gone. Travelling from Montréal over a month ago,
I can't believe they let a stranger into this country.
They didn't admit the Syrian poet scheduled
to lecture at NYU two days before. I small-talked
the Homeland Security officer about his upcoming trip
to Guelph, Ontario, where his wife's from.

Love, another poet once claimed,

could show us from the vase's broken pieces

what's been lost, and what I understood was

that the vase, if put back together,

becomes an unbroken thing we believe

we might lose again, and so we do.

I don't stick to the facts—

what if I wrote lines that took nothing

but the shape of my thoughts?

No irritable reaching for an old story,

no derailed, hanger-on lurk.

A rail bridge connects the old playground

to the abandoned car lot—I say that knowing

I don't have to hand anyone even one more idea on this,

and exactly nobody would be asked to relate,

to say nothing of the woman's fitted wool coat on the seat opposite,

symbol of my fragility or mortality.

Is that poetic license? *It's not something I need to know,*

this man says, then gets up to get coffee.

The sky is now a diluted pistachio green over the Hudson.

They call it stranger's weather.

*I rather think I did ask,* a poem about the river asked.

I asked too—not about a better view;

about someone entirely different, about what remains

after the broken vase is no longer a recognizable vessel.

## Appetites

You wake hearing the girl next door come in at two a.m.
    In the event that it's a ghost, it's telling you
not to waste time in bed
      worrying.
      You should be sleeping, or doing
      anything else.
You haven't yet seen the faun, the red fox,
      or the rabbit.

The statue of a woman in the lily-padded lake is waist-deep,
a mimicry of Diana's animal life, suspicious of sleep.

With her in mind, you're troubled even thinking of things
that don't frighten you.

But this, too, is a waste of time and talent.

There is good slumber
to be sought in the rush of ruminations outside yourself:
    in listlessness of reeds on the dead embankment,
    in languor of bee by a late marigold
        or duck feathers gathering in a corner of falling
        water.

You realize you haven't organized your life.
You've forgotten yourself entirely.
You wake up and try to pick up the thread.

# Jacob McArthur Mooney

**Jacob McArthur Mooney**'s (b. 1983) books are *The New Layman's Almanac*, *Folk*, and *Don't Be Interesting*, each from McClelland & Stewart. He was the Guest Editor of *The Best Canadian Poetry in English 2015*. His work has been shortlisted for the Trillium Book Award in Poetry and the Dylan Thomas Prize, and won the Bliss Carman Award from *Prairie Fire* magazine and the *Arc Magazine* Poem of the Year contest. From 2012-2017, he was the Director of the Pivot Reading Series. Originally from Lunenburg County, Nova Scotia, he now lives in Toronto.

## A Guide to Getting It Right

Rescind your faith
in synonyms. They don't
exist. Understand
                         that language is
like any living creature, a product
of forever-evolution.

And no one suggests that
                         two animals
are the same thing, even when
someone does, they're just
waving at the species with
catch-all categories like
birds, dogs, or bipeds.

            Know how to map out
the space a word makes, how no
part of it is something else at all.
            Put ten properties together
in a sentence, let your nation shape around
the holes you've left unfilled. I had this cat
            growing up that
got hit by a car, my mother said he
went away, then
passed on, and then
died.

## Mapfolk

That the sports team I like best is the most morally defensible,
and the same goes for the country I live in. Fill in the photograph

with agriculture, politics. Unfold the shrinking circles
and have someone tell Greenland the news.

But this imagining is only a comfort to those
born sponsored in its vertices, while a fissure-bleed

of rural routes reigns out its unpaved ripple. Tell me everything:
guess your home against the globe, mark your height

along the wall. Step onto a compass rose centred in a public square
that identifies the distances to sixteen major cities. Break a piece

off your body and bury it to root. Grow an army of witnesses
to walk out all the measurements. Double check everybody's math.

## Golf Pro, Monobloc, *A Theory of the Firm*

I've been told certain seabirds travel inland
bringing cold, bewildered prey. Heavy prey.
Or that airplanes find their pilots' fingers heavy,

so they purge their swollen bellies over grasslands.
Deck chairs, paperbacks, anything. Any lost manifest
can catch the air and zombie feather-headed down

to where it drapes its dead body on the trap by fairway eight,
or the dogleg bend beyond the reach of eager heavyweights.
I didn't used to be like this. I made the college team

on the strength of college arms. Went bald and lost my knee.
I took the job we all take. Weak-winded, undersized,
I still drove the ball far enough to teach lessons.

But now the sky is falling. Every morning brings cast-aside lumps
or lightest finery. A monobloc chair made the tumble unslighted,
hero to its factory cousins turtled under husky sitters.

An eight-iron away, Jensen's *A Theory of the Firm*.
I pulled the chair up to reread it, bent to help
the last Sumatran spider through a crack in its cage.

One summer day: pianos. Dotted obstacles downed as if
they stumbled on a conference of cartoon antagonists.
It went on like this. We ran out to scavenge antique doors

and christening gowns. The club built a house but we moved into
the basement. Played the radio loud to drown out falling parcels.
My game slowed down but we picked up better hobbies.

My daughters learned falconry and fencing. My son wore
the pelts of soft endangered mammals. My wife found the memoirs
of some far-off Casanova and left to learn his language.

On hole four's island, I found a bubble-wrapped trestle desk.
I dropped my clubs, pulled the chair up and my Jensen.
I have lived long enough and there is no one left unlike me.

## The Fever Dreamer

I have made the boys.
Baden boys, Britannia boys. I have made them cruel and handsome,
made them march in single file, backs straight, up on their haunches
like new carnivores.

I have taught the boys
to purge the waste from their lives, to cure their spit-cleansed trousers
of mange and leg and mittens. I've had my boys go post-European
and sew their pockets shut.

I have beaten boys.
I have whipped their heads with eyebrows. I have singed their shirts
and broken out the laxatives. I have proctored international, made
and been remade by boy.

I have told the boys
I Want Them. I want them for King and Kaiser. Want them *Lusitania*
and Sino-Tsarist tensions. Want them cradle of statecraft
and Metternichs and mobs,

want armament contracts
for accommodating fathers, mothers who would pack-mule pamphlets
into bedrooms, the boyish Yes! of Oxford Press, printing (in three
weeks) *Why We Are At War.*

I have become the boys'
sincerity, their sweated-out details. I have boxed the boys,
bent them at their waists and wound their backs for marching.
If you scratch my surface,

I'll be the boys' defence.
I'll settle their wounds with the Good News of Field Dress. I will
wear them hats. I will tie them heads to handkerchiefs. You'll taste how
I have egged them on,

how I've fed the boys
provisions. In those first provocations of union hall and field,
I showed them the fruitful economy of hunters, bought them
the blades for first shaves.

With the saccharine blood
of their comeuppance I have calmed them. I've told them to suckle on
the nearest teat to tongue. I have left them to tend to these friendships
in dark habitats.

The boys, as boys, descend
on repertoires of bravery. I know I bring this up again, but look
at what they're wearing. Observe the benevolent
cotton at their necklines,

their badges and banners
torqued into hieroglyph. Boy at swim. Boy at camp. Boy against
the outline of the nation that protects him. Boy using arrow.
Boys embraced around a flame.

I apologize to Europe
for the invention of the boy. I did not design them to be
tyrants or marauders. I didn't dream them up to die.
I demanded of my boys

that they drift in mythic
packs, wicked on the scent of antagonist or sibling. I regret
that climactic lifting of the fence, my appeal that they factor in
the fattened hearts of kings.

I have brokered boys,
bankrolled their littleness and lust. I've erected border towns
between and inside them, built hives in their minds,
free from history.

## The Next Wave

Cornered in this keyhole
nightmare in Brittany, I've engendered all the boys, as brood
and as bereavement. Call me piper, boogeyman, but it is true
I made the boys.

I have made the boys bewildering.

# Sachiko Murakami

**Sachiko Murakami** (b. 1980) is the author of three collections of poetry: *Get Me Out Of Here* (2015), *Rebuild* (2011), and *The Invisibility Exhibit* (2008). She has been a literary worker for numerous presses, journals, and organizations, and was the 2017 Writer-in-Residence at the University of Toronto. She teaches, edits, and writes in Toronto.

## Portrait of Suburban Housewife as Missing Woman

Mouth open, she looked as though she was protesting
her inclusion. I brought her to a place
where no one speaks. *There's been a mistake,*
she said with the soft folds
of her tracksuit, the car keys
she held like a set of brass knuckles.
*You can't take me anywhere I don't wish to go.*
I did have to drive out of town to take this picture.
As evidence, it was the next day's news.
Now it's so obvious, her clavicle's hard line,
the shadow there, a hollow big enough for two thumbs.

# Wishing Well

My fist holds as many coins
as I can carry. All are stamped with the Queen's effigy;
Elizabeth, D.G. Regina, the resident of pockets,
a woman I've never met though I always know
her whereabouts. Each face pressed
into another person's palm before mine.
The stink of sweat and metal. The waste of it.

I wish for a return, or for justice.
It's safe to do that here. You can throw wishes away
and no one will fish them out
before the park's authority comes to drain the pool
and return the coins to currency.
Maybe I'm buying the future a Coke,
a popsicle, a bag of potato chips, a fix.

Maybe I'm trying to bribe God.
I'm not the type who says no to a panhandler,
or yes.

I scatter my spare change
all at once. Each completes its parabolic reach,
falls dead weight. I wish until the ripples still enough
to show my face: and just beyond, lit stars
bright as found dimes.

## Skipping Stones

I fling flat stones into the surf, corral
my anger in the strangely angled pose.
Each beat's concentric blip a sound so odd
it clarifies the brine to mellow blues.
My mother's ex once skimmed his bottle caps
down at the lake; not littering, I thought,
the glinting disc's fourteen discrete hop-hops.
Now I trust black, the solid strength of rock.
My hand must learn the pebble's weight, and know
which chips will change the shape and spoil the trick;
this can't be accurately guessed, and though
some seem to work without my gauging it;
I fling them to new ocean bottom homes,
and some I leave to dry upon the beach. Skip stones.

# Rebuild

After the unimaginable, what's left: a return to rawness.
The land cracks and swallows. The home,
erased. All knickknacks back to dust. If only

that happened. Instead a neighbour
buys the bicycle, paints it blue. Instead
the graveyard markers are tactfully removed.

Instead names are changed, a farm's,
and the official memory. Now a child born in exile.

Now he becomes a father. Now redress.
Now he's a father, a body. Now ashes.

Now begin.

Now begin again.

## They expanded the Icelandic-food-as-gifts store

*a rawlings, KEF-CDG*

The silvery mouth of Borealis between my legs.

The sudden tongue of black ash where field was meant to be.

The rough edge of Atlantic licked smooth over time.

The bitten edges of loss, of lava. Its mouthful of fine grit.

A gust. A gust, a gale. A gust, a gale, a storm. A gasp.

A candle and another in the dark where the song starts.

A wave thrown to shore, the Atlantic's wet mouth wide with grief.

A hollow in stone where the sound licks out.

And pause in storm to run troubled wave over sea palate.

And ash and *eð* and *þorn* settle on tongue of

a tooth-cracked rock to find inside a flash of quartz, frozen

water, of icefall, of *foss*, *œð*'s wet vowels the mouth wrung out,

swirl *skyr, skyr, skyr* or spoon into gale between midday sheets

a lisped sudden tongue of sea *þorn* to ash of dark *ell* wet with grief

# Alexandra Oliver

**Alexandra Oliver** (b. 1970) is the author of *Meeting the Tormentors in Safeway* (Biblioasis 2013), winner of the 2014 Pat Lowther Memorial Award, and *Let the Empire Down* (Biblioasis 2016), shortlisted for the 2017 Pat Lowther Memorial Award. The co-editor of both Random House/Everyman's *Measure for Measure: An Anthology of Poetic Meters* and Canadian formalist journal *The Rotary Dial*, she has performed her work at festivals and venues worldwide, as well as on CBC Radio, NPR and in the 1998 Paul Devlin documentary *Slam Nation*. Oliver is currently a PhD candidate in English at McMaster University.

## Party Music

*Friends, applaud. The comedy is over.*
        —Ludwig van Beethoven


In '68 a great conductor came
to one small European town. His flat
was right above our Gran's. He reeked of fame,

wore grey ostrich shoes, a beaver hat
tipped on a sweep of hair now going white,
a coat in astrakhan. A man like that

deserved the name of *meister*. Appetite
for drama and excitement won at last;
we wondered what he did, by day and night,

the aura of an enigmatic past
(unknown to us, small girls of six and eight)
now flattened by the neutral atom blast

of Swissness. We could only speculate;
he was a mighty river with no source.
But we had watched him leave the building late:

a sleigh pulled by a giant yellow horse
had scooped him up, a Russian at his side.
An undernourished blonde in mink. Of course.

What more could any human being provide?
We had it figured out. We knew this man
was perfect for a widow, bona fide

salvation for the suffering of Gran,
whose patience was as solid as the stones
on Via Maestra. So we made a plan,

imagined, in soft, out-of-focus tones,
her breathless lurking near the fire stairs.
Notified (a buzz between two phones),

down he'd slink to orchestrate affairs;
although our minds had not digested sex,
we grimly guessed what adults did in pairs.

He'd ring the bell, come in for tea. The next
instalment of our hot imaginings:
her jewelled hands upon his goat-haired pecs,

(insert a full accompaniment of strings)
as preface to the cinematic kiss,
his man-purse chucked aside! Like mighty wings

those sideburns swooped on in. Oh, great abyss
she toppled into, blown by some gust
of sweet, forbidden philharmonic bliss.

All this for romance in the upper crust,
a man above domestic life's dull take,
a Mercury, to whom we pinned in trust

the soft and sparkling trappings of a rake,
all caviar and aftershave, the gold
of damask curtains, opened by mistake.

*Party member*, the phrase of cold
and adult truth was just one part left out
of what the two of us were later told.

It wasn't what we'd hoped to think about,
for party used to mean the happy mess,
the donkey tail, the streamers and the shout,

the ripple of a silver satin dress,
a belch of pink confetti in the air,
but now we heard the coda of distress:

the rattle of a door against a chair,
the flutter of the bitter yellow stars
that, long ago, three cousins had to wear.

No nothing, whether sequin, crumb or shred,
no fur, no silk, no balcony guitars,
the strains of the *Horst Wessel Lied* instead.

Because, of course, the Party wasn't ours.

Alexandra Oliver

# Meeting the Tormentors in Safeway

They all had names like Jennifer or Lynne
or Katherine; they all had bone-blonde hair,
that wet, flat cut with bangs. They pulled your chair
from underneath you, shoved their small fists in
your face. Too soon, you knew it would begin,
those minkish teeth like shrapnel in the air,
the Bacchic taunts, the Herculean dare,
their soccer cleats against your porcine shin,
that laugh, which sounded like a hundred birds
escaping from a gunshot through the reeds—
and now you have to face it all again:
the joyful freckled faces lost for words
in supermarkets, as those red hands squeeze
your own. *It's been so long!* They say. Amen.

## Plans

Mid-morning: here I sit with splayed-out hands,
womanly and worked-with, on the towel.
The manicurist, twenty at the most,
is pretty in her bow-necked carbon dress.
(The shop has not been open for a week;
a box of Thornton's Classics stands uneaten
on the table, by a copy of *Hello!*)
She has a job. Someone has told her so.
If she were made to do it, she's uncertain
(and, if she were uncertain, would she speak?).
Plucking metal clippers from a glass,
she starts to pick away, a little lost,
until the rip, the blood, the muted howl,
*I'm sorry!* Meaning, *Not what I had planned.*

A half an hour before, this girl had told me
how she loved her small-town school back home,
excelled in sciences, rejoiced in donning
lab coats to untuck the life from frogs,
set fire to wide-hipped flasks, lean in to watch
the magnified amoebae wink and burble
coyly in the Petri dish, a hand
unshaking on the arm of her best friend.
A girl's future should be full and bright, a marble,
but (alas for her) there is a catch:
we take on the immediate. Hope flags;
wishing to be wise and come out shining,
we pop a beaker over our own flame.
We do it cheerfully. We do it coldly.

Tamping down the soggy, trembling cotton
on my bleeding cuticle, she asks
*What colour?* Meaning, *How can I do better*
*when I know the business isn't in me?*
Look, I want to say, I've done it too,
sold candlesticks I'd never care to clean,
told women that a lipstick made them young,
gone drinking with the after-hours gang;
I've told admirers things I didn't mean
and said to students, *It'll come to you!*
The wrong direction never treats you kindly.
I long to tell her that it doesn't matter;
there's a way to live and shirk the axe,
though what that is, I've probably forgotten.

## Christopher Robin Kindergarten Class Photo, 1974

There in the front.
That's me in the blazer
and little white hat,
already the poser,

the chin pointed up,
designing my ruse,
all set for disaster
in my red shoes.

# Soraya Peerbaye

**Soraya Peerbaye**'s (b. 1971) first collection of poetry, *Poems for the Advisory Committee on Antarctic Names*, was nominated for the Gerald Lampert Award. Her poems have appeared in *Red Silk: An Anthology of South Asian Women Poets*, the chapbook anthology *Translating Horses*, and various Canadian literary journals. Her book, *Tell: Poems for a Girlhood*, won the 2016 Trillium Book Award for Poetry and was nominated for the Griffin Poetry Prize. She holds an MFA in Creative Writing from the University of Guelph.

# Gorge Waterway

The word that in my mother tongue means throat—
    *gorge*—here,

a glacier-carved passage; the sea, brash,
moving inland, toward

the shirred surrender of the estuary.

Salt marshes; mudflats at the mouths of Craigflower Creek,
Colquitz River; eelgrass meadows.

Throat, and the breasts of birds—*rouge-gorge, oiseau-mouche,
à gorge rubis, moqueur gorge-blanche.*

There had been the tumult of rumour, trials, an overturned
verdict, then silence. A shoaling.

*We could tell by her breathing*, said Warren. So they
knelt by her body, then. Listened.


\*


He testified how her jeans slid from her hips as they dragged her
face-down to the water. Hair darkening

the breadth of her back, her buttocks, the backs of her legs.
Black-grassed meadow.

*Faire des gorges chaudes de quelque chose, de quelqu'un,*
to laugh at something or someone.

Amidst exotic blackberry, thickets of snowberry and Nootka rose:
clusters of white drupes, luminescent, ceremonial;

crimson rosehips on red-thorned stems, blackening
in late fall.


\*


He refused to testify at Kelly's first trial.
Contempt of court. The stuttered drift of tides.

—*What happened then?*
                    —*She started mumbling words.*

Seven years later, he gives us a moment
from the water's edge. An in-between place.

Wanting something to catch those words, wanting
the little lives

that gather what they can by feel.
Feather, fan, siphon; filament and spine.

*Is this possible?* the Crown asked the pathologist. She spoke
of the scalp, *soft and boggy.*

The brain, delicate coral of self. The swelling
cortex. Seizure, speech.


\*


In Warren's telling, she drowns looking up, so that she sees
her assailant through water. Face

blurred, but the hands
clear.

Two girls. One standing, water up to her pelvis. The other
supine, her feet trying to find purchase.

He stood on the shore, he said; saw Kelly raise her arm
then bring it down.

*Open hand*, the edge of her palm.

The pathologist followed the descent of bruise
almost to bone. *The hyoid*. An archaeology of throat.

*Son refus m'est resté dans la gorge*, her refusal
stuck in my craw.

Oysters, shells marking the periphery of their silence. Year
after year. Rough grey rings of secretions without; within,

smooth ligament scars.

\*

In that other telling, the one that must be true, her face
pressed to the estuary floor.

Sand and pebbles, crushed shells. Brackish water. It floods
her mouth, her nostrils.

Exhibit 18, the envelope of small stones taken from her throat.
A teaspoon, said the pathologist. As though speaking

of sugar, salt.

Saltwater, sweetwater, a whirlpool. *Je lui enfoncerai
les mots dans la gorge*, I'll make her eat her words.

Moon on water, pearl and black.
*Red glaze.*

How could he see? *From the moonlight*
*glimmering on the water.*

\*

(In the half-light of the museum, the Aboriginal fishing tool
in its glass case.

*The fish swallows the baited gorge, then tries to spit it out.*
*The gorge*

*turns, wedging in the throat of the fish…*)

\*

I walk with the word in my mouth, because of the cause
of death: not

the skin layer, fatty layer, muscle layer, *sheared*
from each other; not the organs

crushed against the backbone; not
the trauma to the brain.

*The cause of death was drowning.*

His clothes crumpled in the washing machine's
silver drum, the thrum of water.

*Go check Kelly's jacket,* said Warren. *She said her jacket*
*reeked, like blood, like rotten fish.*

# Disque

A boy with whole-bodied intent,
      he'd snatched the 78 rpm
   from the Morning Glory gramophone,

     shattered it: shining blue-black shards
at his feet. This object, known first
   by its breaking.

A grown man, his fingers amble
      the dust jackets, the fine print
   of their spines. A physical musing.

    Not the fumble for cassettes,
the noisy sputter and catch
   of sprockets in the deck's

mechanism. But this—the record held,
      by its edge, at an angle, shirt sleeve
salving the bruise of fingerprints. *Écoute,*

     he says. We sit in the living room, as the needle
passes through its brief darkness, a cyclical,
   crackly creek. We tilt our heads back.

His favorites restored, iridescent on compact discs,
     but he rarely plays them, can't bear
   their breathless perfection,

     misses the scratch, skip and stutter,
that sent us into laughing fits.
   Or perhaps

it's the gesture itself,
     the needle carried to the record's surface,
   a pond where the water ripples inwards.

# James Pollock

**James Pollock** (b. 1968) grew up in Woodstock, Ontario, and studied at York University and the University of Houston. His book *Sailing to Babylon* was a finalist for the Griffin Poetry Prize and the Governor General's Literary Award in Poetry, and won an Outstanding Achievement Award in Poetry from the Wisconsin Library Association. He is the author of *You Are Here: Essays on the Art of Poetry in Canada* and editor of *The Essential Daryl Hine*. His poems have appeared in *The Paris Review, AGNI, Maisonneuve, The Fiddlehead*, and elsewhere. He is Professor of English and Creative Writing at Loras College in Dubuque, Iowa, and lives with his wife and son in Madison, Wisconsin.

## Radio

The kitchen dark, the summer night air warm,
and my father at the kitchen table, radio

turned down low, alone, listening to baseball.
My mother and I come inside from our swim,

toweling off. The crowd is restless. Long silences
between pitches in the play-by-play.

Look how he holds the radio in both hands
like a steering wheel, thumb on the tuning dial

to catch the wavering channel, fighting static.
His eyes glitter like a field of fireflies.

James Pollock

# My Grandmother's Bible

*Mary Pollock, née McConnell (1887-1959)*

The shape, the heft, of a shovelful of sod.
A sheaf of God. Its soft-worn pebbled grain

of supple Levant morocco. Two rips
yawn along the spine two inches long,

a strip of leather's lacking at the top.
The pages, inked in foxed and well-thumbed red

along the fore-edges like a thousand lips,
are gilded on heads and tails, the gilt half-faded.

Out of the biblical plagues of the 1930s,
black storms of dust, vast ravening clouds

of grasshoppers, comes this blasted, smoking heirloom,
a nut-brown flap of torn and weathered leather

wrapping a slab of paper. Its English
plunges into my heart like a small black bird.

## Sailing to Babylon

I sailed a boat to Babylon
and rowed back lonely in the rain.
I struck out down a country lane,
I set my course for Avalon,

but once I'd crossed the Acheron
and slept beside the silver Seine,
I sailed my boat to Babylon
and rowed back lonely in the rain.

I've worshipped at the Parthenon,
I've loved the girls of Aquitaine,
but when they lay my bones in Spain,
O tell the Tetragrammaton
I sailed my boat to Babylon
and rowed back lonely in the rain.

# Prague

Someone had left a mannequin in the street.
It was wearing a wedding dress
and—but no,

it was a woman, standing on a box.
A small crowd had gathered around her
and her eyes were closed.

I hesitated. Then
reached down to the jar at her feet
as if I were bending to pet a stranger's dog.

And as though I had deposited a soul, *chink*,
her eyelids fluttered open,
her fingers flickered,

she awoke like Hermione
astonishing her husband
in the miraculous final scene of *The Winter's Tale*.

Later, through the window of a restaurant,
I saw her dash across a crowded street,
clutching her skirts to keep them from the rain.

# Michael Prior

**Michael Prior**'s (b. 1990) poems have appeared in numerous publications across North America and the UK. His first full-length collection of poems, *Model Disciple*, was named one of the best books of 2016 by the CBC and made year-end lists from *The Walrus, The Rumpus, Vallum*, and the League of Canadian Poets.

# Half

I am all that is wrong with the Old World,
and half of what troubles the New.

I have not seen Spain or the Philippines,
Holland or Indonesia. In the other room,

my grandfather nods off in front
of *Wheel of Fortune.* I have seen his Japan

in photos—the last good suit he wore,
grey, tailored in Kyushu. Believe

Pat Sajak is a saviour: he divines new riches
like water hidden from a dowser's

willow switch, trembling through
unfamiliar territories, proffered

like a makeshift cross. The same faith
should be proof enough

of my current crisis. There was a game
we once played. I'm in it now.

The wheel turns, strobes its starlight
across another centrifuge, that spinning globe,

a kid's finger skimming its surface,
waiting for it to stop. *This is where I'll live.*

# Ventriloquism for Dummies

Pine plosives, alveolar carpentry:
my life, lived like an elaborate glove.
Tilt my head, a pale seashell scribed by lathe,
and listen to the few unfurling thoughts,
the dry shake of dust. *Semper idem*, no?
I loved that girl with the Cheshire-cat grin
inked across the nape of her neck's vellum.
My hinged digits once traced its glow as if
it were a sliver of moon. Nowadays,
she works nights on an alabaster lake.
*My first thought was, he lied in every word,*
and I wasn't wrong. Charlie McCarthy
may be my homeboy, but that suede coffin
became my home. Long dawns in the valley,
I dreamed a redwood forest. At its centre
was another jester with a cheap suit
and misplaced mandible. Drop me, toss me,
and I lie limp: a tidal tryst of bleached
branches, a good joke gone bad, or a line
soured by time. Got wood? It's all I've got.
Try not to notice these synchronized lips,
*that hoary cripple, with malicious eye.*

## Swan Dive

*I was the more deceived.*
        —Ophelia, *Hamlet*, III.i


It's hard to stay angry on a bed of water.
Harder yet to remain above the tide—

hence the anchor, hence the dive.
For those of us who practice our Ophelia,

we creatures of conscience, let it be known
that I have keened the lake in colder

seasons, seen the loves returned by acts
of ice. Olive bottles, agate necklaces

bought in beachfront shops for cheap.
*I shall th' effect of this good lesson keep.*

I rearrange my lost and found. That man
who was discovered rooting the bottom

three decades after his death: in his boat,
a fish still writhed the line. Hear me out.

Even the swans' necks don't shape a heart
when they hunt beneath the dark.

## In Cloud Country

In cloud country, water has but two states:
we focus on the crease between a wave and its cold,
between us and the sun. In cloud country, your mind
settles its mist across the TV's broken screen,
the IV's taped labels, the metal rungs strung
along the bedframe, like ladders into a hidden room.
Here, Kyushu is a doorway left ajar, a nightlight's
shadow shift. Here, we admit ourselves
the paper's ninth and impossible fold—the way
we say *Hello*, meaning, *Hold on a little longer*.
Or, *I don't know*, meaning, *It's true*. Errant cells spill
like sea salt over the corridor's mirrored linoleum,
as we shuffle from floor to floor, and you live
long enough to see your glasses return to style,
your plaid shirts, your knit cardigans. Within our borders,
your hair frays cirrus into sky, while that bride,
so serious in every photo, never had to be you. Drowsy,
draining through a plastic tube, in cloud country,
you say, *That was all so long ago*: each closet,
a mossy gate, each wormwood cabinet, a cabin
dissolving in your nowhere backwoods,
where the plural is story—the singular, skin, and the notice
stapled to the door does not make of one face
many. Was there ever a quiet street, a pink bungalow,
a trio of hunched maples, a cup of cooling sencha
waiting in this nation for you? In cloud country,
you say, *It feels like I'm being eaten*, and choke down
spoonfuls of ice-cream, lemon jello. We thicken
your water with powdered bone. In cloud country,
the horizon doesn't sever the sky, but spills upwards,
a helix of white smoke, burnt leaves. While the fledglings
in our chests bear no desire to leave the nest,
or rot to barbed wire, snagged cloth. At this latitude,
the textbooks declare the heart an un-cracked

robin's egg—the mind, a clever mockingbird's—
and every morning is the morning
you showed us the bitterns, curtained by bulrushes,
towering in their sleep. You closed our eyes
as we passed the one broken on the boulevard.
It is here, in cloud country, that you promise
to reveal how to uncrimp each beak from its paper bud,
how to unfurl each wing with the perfect pressure
of fingers not yet talons, veins not yet tunnels
of wind and sleet. It is here that you mutter, *I had a name*
so that we understand: every animal has wings.
No dignity in indignity, you kept it all to yourself
in cloud country, where the sheets folded you
and the crinkled gown exposed you; where the swallows
never stood still—and never stood
for want. We kept them to ourselves. We kept this
for you. You plead, *Leave a window open,*
*a skylight unlocked.* We flatten our faces
against the glass's double-pane. We couldn't
finish those final folds alone. You left us
for an image of astounding order. There was
no order. We listen to the radio for your whereabouts
until we, too, bear throats wracked by static,
blistered with Coriolis. The fields that stretch
behind the boulevard rise and evaporate easy
from their bedrock—now, no different than bed.
In cloud country, it rains newspaper cranes, it cries
Fujita scale, it hears your tectonic mumble merge
with ours: There is no scale for now and then.
You are the paper's one hundred and third fold,
the nebula's gauzed edge. In cloud country,
you say, *Thank you.* We say, *Thank you.*

## Conditional

Hawk perched on the silo's lip,
a thing unfinished, a thing
of unhinged shadow, which even
when still is still in motion,
skimming the bales, the stalks,
and when you look away, it drops.

# Damian Rogers

Born and raised in the Detroit suburbs, **Damian Rogers** (b. 1972) emigrated to Canada in 2002. She has worked as an arts journalist, literary editor, event organizer, educator, and non-profit director. The author of two books of poetry, *Paper Radio* (ECW Press, 2009) and *Dear Leader* (Coach House Books, 2015), she is working on a memoir due out in 2019.

# Redbird

It's the middle of the night.
I've set the house on fire
with those matches I love,
the ones in the kitchen
with the red bird on the box.
You can strike them anywhere.
*Allumettes qui s'allument partout.*
Take care: may ignite if box is
dropped, shaken, or crushed.
This same bird flies through
a tattoo on your arm.
The house is burning down
and I am thinking of boats.
You hate the matches, the smell
of bent, black spoons.
I light one and it falls to the floor.
Another and another. Take care.
I don't know what to save
from this place, sailing from wall
to wall, room to room, smoking.
You are not here. You are rain
battering against some window.
I don't know what to save.
The red bird eats everything in sight.

Damian Rogers

# Snake Handler

No tricks,
I just love them
as my own blood

and keep my eyes
on the ceiling.

O Brothers, I sing,
your bodies are thick

as wrists, your skins
my only book.

I relieve them
of poison,

I undo what they do.
I'm charcoal and paper.

Touch me: I leave
a mark on your hand.

This is just costume,
my Depression dress,
my buckled shoe.

Tin flowers in my ears
play spiral-groove blues.

## Song of the Last Shaker

One line,

       two line,

              three line,

                     plane.

I skate across the lake on a bone-made blade.

My spine is an arrow, a leg of His chair.

My nose straight and narrow and long
                  as my hair.

My body's for bruising.

My heart is her sky.

I train my breath
        upwards.

I practice.

I die.

Damian Rogers

# The Trouble with Wormholes

How many times must I learn the lesson of compression?
Let go of everything you know and start from scratch.
One friend performing backbends on a beach while another
snaps his tibia on an icy patch of Saskatchewan. I don't think
I'm suffering, my days a series of unexpected gifts punctuated
by a blast of the family rage shot deep into my soft plexus.
It occurs to me I don't have to be so many people. If you're staying
alive spinning stories, it's suddenly a skill that you talk too much.
I'm not sure it's smart to unlock the portal. The reformed raver
claimed he saw my inner wheels spin. Red Cloud, are there wars
where you are? Your great-great-grandson appeared on *Democracy
Now!* with a plan. Will my generation be remembered for anything
I haven't forgotten? They mine the hills for gold, they mine the hills
for uranium, and all around the world, columns are cracking.
I've watched you soar all day. Please teach me how you do that.

## Good Day Villanelle

You ran naked out the door.
The neighbours laughed; I chased you down.
I hardly see you anymore.

I know you're busy.
Did I tell you when you were little how
you ran naked out the door?

You got halfway down the street
before I caught you in my arms.
I hardly see you anymore.

I think I told you this before:
I was giving you a bath and then
you ran naked out the door.

It happened fast.
The neighbours laughed.
I hardly see you anymore.

You have to watch a baby close.
I remember once—

You ran naked out the door.
I hardly see you anymore.

# Johanna Skibsrud

**Johanna Skibsrud** (b. 1980) is the author of two novels: *Quartet for the End of Time* and the Scotiabank Giller Prize winning *The Sentimentalists*. She is also the author of a collection of short fiction, *This Will Be Difficult to Explain, and Other Stories* (2012; shortlisted for the Danuta Gleed Award), and three collections of poetry: *Late Nights With Wild Cowboys* (2008; shortlisted for the Gerald Lampert Award), *I Do Not Think That I Could Love a Human Being* (2010; shortlisted for the Atlantic Poetry Prize), and *The Description of the World* (2016; shortlisted for the Pat Lowther Award, winner of the Canadian Authors Association Award for Poetry and the Fred Cogswell Award). Skibsrud is an Assistant Professor of English at the University of Arizona where she teaches modern and contemporary poetry, and poetics. She and her family divide their time between Tucson and Cape Breton, Nova Scotia.

## I'd be a Hopper Painting

It's just this: that I'd like things not to end.
That I'd never get past morning if I could.

I'd be a Hopper painting. Freight Cars, Gloucester, 1928.

Or, if I had to be a Summer Evening, in 1947,
I wouldn't be the girl. I'd be the
step by the rail of the porch; I wouldn't
listen to the man.

Or wonder if the girl will turn; forgive him, and take him in.

Cape Cod Morning, 1950, for example: I wouldn't be the woman
leaning from the well-lit room. Instead, I'd be the pane of glass
and look (but not like her, out to the yard and waiting—
for what, for whom),

inside and out at once, without desire.

I wouldn't even be a shadow if it touches her. I wouldn't risk it.
I would stay away from women.

I'd be the lamp on the bridge of the Manhattan Loop,
in 1928. The point where the sand meets the grass at the
Wellfleet shore. The red wheel that sits out back
of the Panet River place. The square of light on the wall.
The unseen bow of the yawl that is hidden by a
sudden swell, in 1935. I'd be the diagonal thrust of the
Shoshone cliffs, I'd be the bright rock face that's set in
stark relief by a black shadow cast in 1941.

If, let's say, on a summer's evening a girl forgives a man,
might not she, in waking, find herself inside
another—a Cape Cod—morning,
three years gone, and set to staring there?

I'd be a Hopper painting if I could.
Even his women he paints solid.
But I wouldn't be a woman.
I'd be Freight Cars, Gloucester, 1928.
I'd be the light on the slanted grass.

## I do not think that I could love a human being

I do not think that I could love a human being; I would not
know it if I squeezed too hard. I would be a great bear. I would
go rumbling through.

I would try to eat you. I would stand alone,
in the quiet centre of you, and roar. No, I
could not love you. I could not
love a human being.

I would get so
stuck on things. The small

flaws in you, like

the way that you will die;
it would stick in my throat, I could not love you.

And the way that, if you touched me, I would be
as if to you a solid object,
as if a boot, a stick, a stone.

And you to me. The way that I could

pick you up. That I could
hammer you against me; that I could
bruise myself on you, and still have only a

brief impression of you left there on my skin.

And, if I cried, that too would be
an imitation of the thing that I would feel.

And the pain itself, if it were real, would come as if
so separately from you that it might

equally have been a whip, a rope,
a rail with which I thrashed myself when I

thrashed myself with you.

No, I could not love a human being if they
could not leave a mark.

Even if I were a bear
and I ate you, you would
move right through me.

Even if you were a bear
and you ate me, I would
move right through you.

But I am not a bear. And will not eat you.
If I said I could, I could not.

And you are not a bear. And will not eat me.

And that is why I could not love you.
And that is why I could not love you.
And that is why I could not love you.

# Mast

Uprooted, it's a heavy, awkward thing.

Ed and I, at bow-watch, look for rocks,
and shallow ground.

An osprey wings by.

A seal, curious,
follows at some distance.

Under the bridge it's
cool and dark, and when we yell—
just one long note—we hear it
resonate, rib to rib, inside.

Once more in open air,
Ed and I do a dance up on the rail,
And lean into the wire.

Then he bends, picks
seaweed from the hull,
and turns,

wears it like a moustache; his
lip squeezed to his nose.

*I'll pay you Tuesday, for a hamburger today,*
he says, bowing. Extending,

generally, a hand.

## "Come and See the Blood in the Streets!"

As the form of a flame. Less form than flame.

As bells, as clocks, as trees… As a shout,
a held breath. As the bursting of geraniums…

The world enters, intrudes. Becomes, again,
what it already was.

The thought precedes it as a hand precedes the word—
only afterward leaving its mark.

So that even if, in being drawn against that distance,
an explanation fails; is only this: a line, so brief as to be
invisible to the eye—as that behind an ascending bird,
which is, in the moment of its seeing, already gone…

Then it is that. Or at least the question left in that wake.

Beyond, there is just—a sheet of light against the sky.

As Pablo Neruda once wrote: "All the blood of the children
ran through the streets like the blood of children," as literal
as that.

As though a thought, derived from no source, had, at every
moment, already emerged.

The heart pierced through, the question trailing.

# Souvankham Thammavongsa

**Souvankham Thammavongsa** (b. 1978) is the author of *Small Arguments* (2003), winner of the ReLit Award, *Found* (2007), the basis for a short film that screened at TIFF and Dok Leipzig, and *Light* (2013), winner of the Trillium Book Award for Poetry.

# Materials

Growing up, I
did not have books


The only reading material
there was

were old newspapers laid out
on the floor

to dry
our winter boots

or wrap
things of glass


When I learned to read,
the winter boots

lay dripping
in the hallway;

the glass, broken
and uncovered

because I knew this
this

would be my way in

*Water will never lie to you...*
  —Gwendolyn MacEwen, "Water"

## Water

  will lie to you,
      make you believe
          this

    unmarked end
        isn't deep

  —until you go in

    without enough air

       to find your way back

  It breaks light
      before light knows

       where it is

     and takes shape,

       uncertain of is own:

          in the palm of a hand,

     a glass lifted to drain

If you wait long enough,
　　　　　you can watch it give up

　　　　　　　　　　its grooves, its scars

keeping warm cold—

　　　　　losing itself

　　　　　　　　　　in what it didn't want, to become

## At the Farm

I was sitting in the car counting the black flies

They had come in through the open window

There were four

One was on the rear-view mirror

The other three were perched on my left hand

I heard a gunshot by the barn and thought nothing of it

We were at a farm

I saw a cow come charging forward with its head half gone

A man with an axe came running behind it

He hit it once

Once he hit it

And it fell to the ground

Everything was eaten

Its eye appeared in a soup that night

Everything accounted for

## **B a r e**

It means you are light, that you can begin differently now, that you've taken it all off

It means to show your tooth and claw, without the work, the polish, the appointment

If the ending were different, if you placed the last letter right after the beginning, it would be an animal, a power, a warning from which to stay away

Face to face, maybe you'd see they're really not all that different, both just trying

A rearrangement, a shift, a move out of place, a spine realigned

But it would take that wouldn't it? That face to face, to know

# Nick Thran

**Nick Thran** (b. 1980) is the author of three collections of poems: *Mayor Snow, Earworm* (winner of the 2012 Trillium Book Award for Poetry), and *Every Inadequate Name*. After an itinerant thirty-six years across Canada, the United States, and Spain, he has settled, along with the poet Sue Sinclair, in Fredericton, NB, where he is father to Abigail and a poetry editor with Brick Books.

## Seriously, It Was the Biggest Cricket

I should have propped something else beside it—
an empty can, or the last half of my sandwich.
As it stands, the cricket's size grows in the telling,
spreads like the news, years ago, of abandoned stacks
of dirty magazines stowed at the creek behind
the street where I grew up. When my bicycle tires
edged over the lip, boys were already clutching the rain-
soaked pages in their fists, the ink of my first
glimpses of flesh were already starting to pale,
to bleed into the leaves. Seriously, we'd say
in the schoolyard, it was the coolest. Later, actual

clothing would melt off actual flesh; yes, melt,
not just fall to the floor, because, seriously, she
was the hottest. Then gossip flares up in the yard's
kindled corners. When she finally calls up, crying,
I don't relay how her *how could yous* clutched
at my throat, pinned me to the receiver, silent, ashamed,
because I knew I'd been the worst.

Then what? I left, took a few bum jobs
humping rich peoples' luggage, spent two years
in Seoul, Korea, navigating through crowds
where, for the first time, I was the tallest,
so I stuck out to this gorgeous backpacker
who speaks fluent Italian, recites whole blocks
of the Inferno aloud, and moved in with her
as soon as I came home, because, seriously,
it felt like the real thing. Though I'm no longer sure

"real" is the right word, because it's years on,
and I'm no longer sure of this house, or this town,
or my job, and with her, lately, well let's just say
this stretch has been tough. So I stuff the last three
cans of a six-pack, a camera, and a sandwich
into a knapsack, set out to hike along a creek
where leaves brushing against my bare forearms
still feel erotic. Rambling, I turn this corner to find

there, on a bare patch of dirt, the world's biggest cricket,
this freakishly massive thing, and clutch at my mouth
as the air fills with the orchestral swell of its legs,
and gather myself enough to snap a single photo
before it leaps so high I think it must be heading
into someone else's life. *Shit*, I whisper further on,
realizing my shot on the bare patch will show nothing
of its largeness. Hear myself having to try to explain,
struggling, because it was amazing, and, seriously,
I've never been able to help myself. One way or another,
I will have to try to tell her every single thing.

# Earworm

So there's likely a more accurate name
for the glow of a deer's eyes in the dark.
For the hunger that drew a python in Florida
to swallow an alligator whole. For the aura,
the swell just before the gut burst.
For why you've been staying up late at night
on a search engine, looking for all of the possible
names for a lump at the back of your nostril.
For the name of that girl who sold you a pill
from the basket of her bike, and rode off while
her fairy wings flapped in the breeze. And a name
for that breeze. Repetune, ohrwurm,
the last song stuck in your head
which became something else. And for what else?
For not being able to say the one thing
that might have kept you from continually falling apart.
For discovering late. For replaying the video clip
of Joltin' Joe Carter's ninth-inning blast
in the '93 series. For the sound when the ball
hit the bat, and everyone knew they'd won
before it left the park. And for the white noise
that isn't white noise, but a poor translation of what
the blood tries to say. And what the blood tries to say.
For the feeling of never wanting to leave the party
and then having to leave. For the ache in your legs
when you should have cabbed home, but decided to walk
and the walk was too far. But you had to keep on—
Earworm, Little One, chugging along, traveling towards a name.

Nick Thran

# Mayor Snow

The mayor's accountant was as humourless
as a glass of snow.

A glass of snow was on the lawn.

The tongues of the deer
are the tongues of the gods
according to local legend.

The deer, growing brave,
dipped their little tongues into the glass
while the mayor's accountant
holidayed with his shame.

He put a gun to his mouth
as the sun shone in Boca Raton.

Snowfall continued at home.
The mayor's spiel was the same.

## Seven Cicadas

1.

Insect bohemian of Aesop—
drum circles through the summer while

the ant hoards
a winter's worth of food

2.

Noisy Weeds of Middle Ground
Happy Blanks
Zealot's Fears
Agents of the Muse

3.

Such reverb
in the belly of the ark
not one creature would have kept

their sanity intact

4.

The ear on a loop
of Aerosmith albums

Just stop      I'll tell you anything
Just stop

5.

It's in high temperatures
and deep exhaustion
that its pitch is in full bloom

6.

Fresh
from the long-haired weeping willow

it lands on window screens as though designed
by government robotics labs
to flush us from our rooms

7.

It thrives on its own emptiness
It never has to choose

# Daniel Scott Tysdal

**Daniel Scott Tysdal** (b. 1978) is the ReLit Award winning author of three books of poetry, the poetry textbook *The Writing Moment: A Practical Guide to Creating Poems* (Oxford University Press), and the TEDx talk, "Everything You Need to Write a Poem (and How It Can Save a Life)." Tysdal's work has appeared in numerous journals and anthologies, including *Poetry, Best Canadian Poetry*, and *Best Canadian Essays*, and has earned him a number of honours, including the Anne Szumigalski Poetry Award and honourable mention at the National Magazine Awards. He is an Associate Professor at the University of Toronto Scarborough.

Daniel Scott Tysdal

# A▸◂B (A MAD Fold-In Poem)

**A▸**                                                          **◂B**

If all we are is

form, then folding in and folding out defines

the simplest fury of our clipped momentum,

and all life is deserted on a list of possible

hiding places for things inside of other things.

God is the unfolding of disbelief's failure

to outwit the demand for the infinity

of a larger voice enfolded in bunches of a more

fragile breathing. Death is felt as the folding of

nothing into the paths the present ploughs under,

enclosures surrendered to enclosures, like mind

as the first model for incarceration opening

up the possibility for profiles of tortured

mobility, or the belief that the moon

is some crazed fire ripped from the sky

on a moonless night and stuffed down

the throat of every enemy – until their

only and irreverent gift to the world is the least

tangible example of silence for the far-reaching

force of the speaking few. Love is the faintest feats

of hate folding tight around an impossible

adoration for distance. Hate

is love folding away from the hope

for some truncated distance, like a poem

as the folding-in fingers which, in closing,

escape their fisty fixity and dissolve into the briefest

palm. A poem

**A▸**                                                          **◂B**

265

# The Walls

*Composed November 9, 1989, on the occasion of the commencement of the Global Wall Project. The first phase involved expanding the Berlin Wall and constructing similar walls in fifty cities, including Tokyo, London, and New York.*


We cannot act until we have all the facts.

We will never have all the facts. We act.
We expand the wall. We found others.

They are living breathing streets, walls
are. This fact arouses us to erect wall
after wall. We think only of the walls.

We think of the walls as stitches
in a blown apart body. The stitches
bring this body back together. The walls,
embracing the globe, will do the same

for us. If not, we will work until every
body is walled off from every other
body. Think of the thrill we'll feel

when we tear down those walls, excited
by the sudden wall of bodies or the joy

of building all those walls anew.

Daniel Scott Tysdal

# Sonnet 155

*Composed on the occasion of the publication of Dr. Marjorie Rubright's* Not To
Be: How One Forgotten Man Made the Globe. Oxford: OUP, 2014.

One ray of light does not the dark curtail.
No hunger's fed by apricots alone.
A solitary wolf's predation fails
to carve a path. The body's more than bone.
Yet Rubright claims a candle is a sun,
asserting Globe's Grand Players did not write
their ageless plays and poems; Shakespeare's the one.
She bids our bard collective a lone good night.
Or does she wake us to a truer flaw?
Our grasp of authorship was far too cramped:
a sonnet's lines by lovers' eyes are drawn,
by royals, stars, and blood the plays are stamped
  and sing, "*totus mundus agit* art;
  in each great work we all compose a part."

## Last Poem

*Pad kākagati* sanctioned, *Year 0, by the Democratic Kampuchea Global Party leadership.*

This, the last poem,
etched in this stone
beneath your feet,
was authored so
we don't repeat
the evil reaped
and sown by verse.

This poem's the last
of our dark past;
now we may curse
with steps the forms
that scorned with words
our work, made lures
of lie-wrought lyres.

Stomp out this poem.
Its lines are brome,
our march pure fire.
From work to sleep,
don't read or tire:
tread smooth the choir
this last trace hides.

Work's only need
is work. Land feeds,
not words. Dream's sigh
is rotten wood,
a hood, sliced eye.
The hog must die
because it's meat.

# Sheryda Warrener

**Sheryda Warrener** (b. 1978) is the author of two poetry collections: *Hard Feelings* (Snare, 2010) and *Floating is Everything* (Nightwood, 2015). Her work can be found online or in print in *Event, Grain, The Fiddlehead, Hazlitt, The Believer*, among others. In 2017, she was the recipient of *The Puritan*'s Thomas Morton Memorial Prize for poetry. Originally from Grimsby, Ontario, she lives in Vancouver, where she's a lecturer in the Creative Writing program at UBC, and facilitates Artspeak Gallery's *Studio for Emerging Writers*.

## Through the Restaurant Window

I can see from where I sit
a freight train going by, rolling forward
in the dark. I can't tell if it's one long train
or a dozen—I close my eyes, listen.

A freight train going by, rolling forward
as our conversation backs up, bridges one gap
or a dozen. I close my eyes, listen.
There are gates within us, you say,

as our conversation backs up, bridges a gap.
You reach across the table, take my hand.
There are gates within us, you say
again. You're right, there's always a distance.

You reach across the table, take my hand
in the dark. I can't tell if it's one long train.
Again, you're right, there's always a distance.
I can see from where I sit.

## We Bought a Little City

First, we remove the dreadful yellow awnings from the shop-fronts in the square. Brighten the streetlamps. Play our instruments for the dairy cows crowding the fence. We angle for more daylight, fill out the appropriate paperwork. Get down on hands and knees to clean out the ditches. We eat breaded fish for lunch, drink a cold beer, volunteer to play our part. No one complains of their dreams or dread. A mangy dog comes out of the forest covered in mud and stinking of deep time. Belonging to the old owners, he wants nothing to do with us, knows we'll use him as a bridge: *Look, there he goes with a pheasant in his mouth.* Late October, the windows display ornamental gourds, tidy piles of leaves. Evening in the forest, the eyes and mouths of jack-o-lanterns spark. A bark, a souvenir. Way off the earth the moon muscles in, entirely invincible.

## A Sudden Gust

*after* A Sudden Gust of Wind (after Hokusai) *by Jeff Wall*

Forget about Hokusai for a minute: in this photograph,
the bend of the tree is a replica of the bend

of the river. A woman loses her headscarf.
A businessman and a farmer crouch into

the wind. Loose-leaf whipped from
a briefcase whirls upward, tangles

with clouds. No sixteenth-century rice field:

this is a cranberry farm outside
Vancouver, actors lurching into the gust.

A digital composite made
of 100 photographs taken over a year. Nothing

can substitute the single brushstroke of
Fuji, so there's no mountain.

Now, lift a corner and let fly

the part of you that can't help
but destroy things. Disrupt

the tableau with a minor catastrophe

and watch the players clutch
at hats, some semblance of

the original: peasants winding through
dry grass, tissues drawn

from a kimono pocket flying skyward.

What did the woman say to the cloud?
*You're the doughy center to this storm.*

The grass whispers, *Rice*

*is nice rice is nice.* Heart and mind
agree on one thing: when seeking a pattern, subvert

the pattern. Ancient Indonesian temple-makers always

turned one stone's marking in the opposite
direction. Nothing's perfect is what

the stars declared, and Borobudur
is circumambulated to this day. This poem

is spliced together from a hundred thoughts, most likely
a modern version of some old idea.

Like the man whose toupée is whipped off, we need to
get over ourselves. Let the wind separate us

from our belongings. Walk empty-minded

into the cranberries and rainwater. Look how
the rectangles of paper become sky! It makes sense now

why the mountain's not there. *Irreplaceable,*
we say to our disoriented selves, this landscape backdrop.

# Self-Portrait: *Cassiopeia I*

*after Joseph Cornell*


Sky chart, painted wood, four apertif glasses, marbles, plaster

head, painted cork ball, metal rods, brad nails, painted

glass. I'm layered in

like light, or something heavier, glue.

Suspended from 26 or 6 pieces

of string. Silk skirt belonging now

to the room, its chlorinated lambent glow

from the silent picture on loop.

Projector overhead sighs through its gills.

Verticality of this skirt, it's everything

I'm made of in this moment. And this desire to last

finds a material place in the loop

the artist makes of time. I become a part

of the soundless dark theatre

and play out my role as any good actor would.

To the average passerby, I look alive.

Sheryda Warrener

# Self-Portrait: *Nimbus II, 2012*

*after Berndnaut Smilde, after Heather Christle*


This cloud is designed

to move like a cursor from one side of the room to the other

This cloud is designed to float inside

uncorrupted by weather

                  This cloud is easy to capture

and won't last forever

The cloud exists without a wonder

of what anyone thinks      We study

the cloud to learn this indifference    little deadpan filibuster

The cloud makes a sudden diagonal

                move to the corner

       The crowd fills the space

attempts to mimic its very nature

as if one  (just by watching)  might gain

       a foothold

knowing "The End" placard

is mounted in the not-so-

distant future

# Ian Williams

**Ian Williams** (b. 1979) is the author of *Personals*, shortlisted for the Griffin Poetry Prize and the Robert Kroetsch Poetry Book Award; *Not Anyone's Anything*, winner of the Danuta Gleed Literary Award for the best first collection of short fiction in Canada; and *You Know Who You Are*, a finalist for the ReLit Prize for poetry. He was named as one of ten Canadian writers to watch by CBC. Williams completed his Ph.D. in English at the University of Toronto and currently teaches in the Creative Writing program at the University of British Columbia. He was the Canadian Writer-in-Residence for the University of Calgary's Distinguished Writers Program. His first novel, *Reproduction*, is forthcoming from Random House.

# Not Saying

Fists in our sleeves, we reach our limit. No way
past Lake Ontario, nothing else to do
until you say the thing you need to say.

Sweeten it if you like. Stir in a name.
It's only talk and we've talked our heads to
foam before, testing the limit in a way.

Like the last time our four feet inched partway
over the city's ledge. Lightheaded you
started to say something you needed to say

then started again, *We could– we can fly one way.
Right over the lake.* How you said it, as if we were two
wild geese, no credit limit in the way. Ain't no way,

I said. *Way.* No way. *Way.* Tonight at the lake
your courage fails again. Knuckles in your pits, you
flap your arms and squawk. Say what you're dying to say.

Of course, don't. We're getting carried away.
We'll stay this side of Lake Ontario, clenched. *Nous
sommes à la limite de l'amitié* – find a way
to translate. If you won't say, I won't say.

## Triolet for you

There is no synonym for *you*.
A billion names for men like me
and none for you. *None*. Not a few.
There is no synonym for you.
The thesaurus says, *No match. Do
you mean yogi?* May I use *thee?*
No, there is no synonym for you.
A billion names for men like me.

Ian Williams

## He will tell me later the story of the woman he has been alluding to all day

because it takes three hours and gives him the blues bad
so not now, not now, later, he promises, then falls asleep
on my couch, shrugging his upper lip like a horse.
Open parenthesis. She wore black dresses. They drank a lot
of Beaujolais. She had been to Europe several times.
Spoke another language, French most likely. Worked
for a firm. Had a way of playing with her earlobes
when searching for words. They did not touch. He held
open doors. She had a son. Divorced, divorcing the father.
The father was still involved. *So you understand*, she said.
*Right right right,* he said. They talked about their money.
They talked about Gare Saint-Lazare. They talked about her
son's teacher. They talked about maybe. There was a moment
in his car when nothing happened. A moment when he thought.
Nothing happened. She leaned toward his lips. *Rien.*
She pulled her earlobe. Closed parenthesis. He doesn't know
where he is or what time it is when he wakes up and he has a long
drive and a trustees' meeting in the morning so not now, not now,
next time, he promises, and gets his harmonica and goes.

## Missed connections: Walmart automotive dept—w4m—(Lunenburg MA)

You. At the Tire and Lube Express. You said lube
and I—did you notice?—revved. Your name tag
was missing so I read your hair, curled like a string of e's,
your forearms drizzled with soft hairs like a boy's
first moustache. Apart from that, you were built
like a walrus. The kind of man that drives a Ford
pickup. Black or silver. You said, *There might be a gas leak*
*and We can't fix that here, but don't worry, we'll get you fixed.*
By *fixed* you meant *hooked up*, by *hooked up* you meant
*in touch with* and meant nothing beyond *touch.*

Me. Volvo. Smelled like gasoline: I overfilled the tank
before the oil change. I took the package that comes
with a filter replacement. Have you already forgotten me?
I had trouble with the debit machine. Remember? You said,
*Turn your card the other way*—remember?—and took my hand,
not the card, took my hand with the card in it
and swiped it through. Remember. Please.
The gasoline. The woman almost on fire.

Ian Williams

# Corrections

*for Dave Kendricken*


I'm sorry. No. A boy, a man falls fell falls fell
from a, the balcony of his apartment building.
A man I know, used to know, when, years ago, back when
he was what was what was something, a colt, a mountain
goat, but human.
                    An accident, they, she, his girlfriend,
his ex-girlfriend, maybe by now, told me, called to tell me,
texted me. *Sorry to have to tell you this by text.* It happened
like that this morning, that morning. That happened
that morning. About this time. Sorry to have to tell you,

someone, one of his friends, the one you know about
as well as I, with the name, the clouds for hair and eyes,
the cloud for voice, that friend was there that morning when
the waves were coming in like Arabian stallions when
he rained the sea was sweating in the sun when
a splash quite unnoticed. The ploughman may have heard
the splash, the forsaken cry.

                    I ache sometimes from loving
this world so much, for loving, I ache sometimes for this
cat's black sweatshirt, for sweat above—the word
gone from me—above—just gone from me—his lip, red eczema
creeping up his neck, tumbling down his arm. Sorry. No. I had it
all, had the, his ending all wrong. Philtrum. Un homme, un tom
beau, il tombe, est tombé, tombe, est tombé.

# Catriona Wright

**Catriona Wright** (b. 1985) is a writer, editor, and teacher. She is the author of *Table Manners* (Véhicule Press, 2017). Her poems have appeared in *Prism International, Prairie Fire, Rusty Toque, Lemon Hound, The Best Canadian Poetry 2015*, and elsewhere. She has been a finalist for the Walrus Poetry Prize, *Arc Poetry Magzine*'s Poem of the Year Contest, and a National Magazine Award. In 2014, she won *Matrix Magazine*'s LitPop Award. She is the poetry editor for *The Puritan* and a co-founder of Desert Pets Press.

# Instinct

*after Delmore Schwartz*

I'm not a sloppily stoppered howl,
not a bear in heat trampling ferns for a world of candy
and rage sex. No, I paid someone to siphon the venom
from my ovaries, to destink my pits. The doctor assured me
it was routine surgery, just a few clean snips
to guarantee I won't be tempted to devour
my young. It's over. It's so over. It's been over
seven years since that animal-ectomy.

But I'm still haunted by the beast I might have become.
Sometimes, I dream of potent dung, of crashing
with pure terror through the slippery and scorn-
fueled city. I dream of feathery antennae combing the air
for mates, of tentacles surging from my chest.
I dream I'm a sheep degrading myself for pellets, an all-knees lamb
falling slickly out of me. I awake screaming,
a hand pressed between my legs.

I chase those musky women who rejected the doctor's advice,
those who never tamped down their ribbits
and warbles, those with tails and stench and an endless
amoral hunger, those who will drag their tumorous bodies
into the desert to die. I sit next to them at parties.
I want to feel my skin scraping off
on their rough tongues. I want to suckle, to be stung.
I corner them and jabber praise. They ignore me,
but I can't stop myself.

## Gastronaut

I would cut off my own thumb for the perfect thimbleful
of wood-ear mushroom and bamboo shoot soup.

My paychecks all go to heirloom parsnips and pickled lamb tongues.
I dream of singed pigs' feet, pearly cartilage and crisp skin.

When Cassie posted those pictures of barbecued tarantulas in Cambodia
I wept with jealousy and rage. It took days and days of foraging
for edible moss just to calm myself enough to sleep.

The candied foie gras is better at Jean Georges than at Mona.
For blocks of congealed chicken blood your best bet is Paz and Petunia.
They churn their own butter.

After I ate my first durian, I didn't brush my teeth for a week.
My breath smelled as though I'd been fellating a corpse.
I coughed on everyone.

I just chose to care about this instead of something else. My life is now
tuned to bone marrow donuts and chef gossip. I'm useless
at any other frequency. At times I'm rancid with resentment,

my body a kingdom of rot. I envy the cavemen their mammoths.
The cannibals their hearts. Lord knows what sumptuous
grubs those elitist toucans gorge themselves on in the Amazon.

White sage and turtle flipper. Turmeric and veal pancreas.
Pine needle and antler velvet. I guess it's as noble and as pointless
and as thrilling and as painful as any other passion.

All my friends are probably off somewhere right now laughing
and slurping bird's nest soup while I sit here rearranging items
on my bucket list, slipping silkworms into the top slot.

My death row meal is a no-brainer: slow-roasted unicorn haunch and deep-fried fairy wings with chipotle mayo dipping sauce.

## Yelp Help

i.

That pub is a bog
standard old man boozer.
The stools are unswivelable.
The music, a classic rock slop
bucket. The taps are busted,
rusted, gunked so bad
the beer tastes like cream
of cauliflower soup. The bartender
is a cad and a bounder,
that is to say, cute.
He has a tattoo on his left shoulder
of me at age two,
my new tiara slipping off
my new head. I beg you,
go anywhere else instead.

ii.

That bar is mason jars
and noise. The boys are all feminists
who adore porn and play ukuleles.
The ladies are all burlesque dancers
who love hurling and burly caber tossers.
Everyone knows each other from science
camp or Twitter. One wall is tulip petals,
another bicycle pedals. The shots are ample.
Burps fill the air with dinner samples.
They serve late night liver
and onions, pots of Earl Grey tea.
I've never been there. I'm afraid if I go,
I'll be so comfortable I'll never leave.

iii.

That club is a saxophone
solo, the phoned-in sexiness
of men in velvet fedoras and women
in red dresses. You can feel the air
feeling you up. Roses are sold in singles.
Singles mingle with the desperation
of babysitter-bought freedom.
The drinks cost you a firstborn.
The muted horn reminds you
how formal love used
to sound.


iv.

That restaurant is macho chefs
taunting each other and showing off
their knife sets. Joon Min
works in the kitchen. He makes a mean
foie gras and plum crostini,
but whenever I see him I remember
how dumb I was to think
loving canapés
a good enough reason
to marry him.

v.

That diner is a front
for an all-girl gang of giggle dealers. I mean,
the waitresses are dimple models who
serve slices of pie a la mode
with sides of MDMA. A coven
of Jolenes. Each temptress smells like
oven-baked bread and deviant sex.
I would eat only ashes
for the rest of my life if it meant I could lift
one of their eyelashes on my fingertip,
hold it before pursed lips.


vi.

Even the garden salad at this place
could clog a mammoth's arteries.
Paper placemats unfold
into pirate treasure maps. The plates
are plastic. The glasses are plastic.
The cutlery and cheese are plastic.
The plastic is an estrogen hoax.
Waiters there wear nametags and gag
props: Frankenstein bolts,
Flintstone bones, an arrow entering
and exiting at the temples. It is a temple
to bottom feeders and bottomless Cokes,
to our society's craven complacency.
But if you have your heart set, I can
cut you a deal. My mother and I,
we own the place.

# Permissions

## Jordan Abel

"uninhabited" taken from *Un/inhabited*. Vancouver, British Colombia: Talonbooks, 2014. Reprinted with the permission of the publisher.

"From *Injun*" taken from *Injun*. Vancouver, British Colombia: Talonbooks, 2016. Reprinted with the permission of the publisher.

## James Arthur

"Distracted by an Ergonomic Bicycle", "Omnivore", "On Day and Night" and "The Sympathy of Angels" taken from *Charms Against Lightning*. Port Townsend, Washington: Copper Canyon Press, 2012. Reprinted with the permission of The Permissions Company, Inc., on behalf of Copper Canyon Press, www.coppercanyonpress.org.

"A Local History" reprinted with the permission of the author.

## Billy-Ray Belcourt

"The Cree Word For a Body Like Mine is Weesageechak," "God's River" and "Love is a Moontime Teaching" taken from *This Wound is a World*. Calgary, Alberta: Frontenac House, 2017. Reprinted with the permission of the publisher.

## Linda Besner

"Mornings with the Ove Glove™", "Villeneuve Villanelle" and "Water Glass" taken from *The Id Kid*. Montreal, Quebec: Véhicule Press, 2011. Reprinted with the permission of the publisher.

"Feel Happier in Nine Seconds" taken from *Feel Happier in Nine Seconds*. Toronto, Ontario: Coach House Books, 2017. Reprinted with the permission of the publisher.

# Shane Book

"Homecoming" taken from *Ceiling of Sticks*. Lincoln, Nebraska: University of Nebraska Press, 2010. Reprinted with the permission of the University of Nebraska Press.

"African Evening" and "Mack Daddy Manifesto" taken from *Congotronic*. Toronto, Ontario: House of Anansi Press, 2014. Reprinted with the permission of the publisher.

# Suzanne Buffam

"Happiness Is Not the Only Happiness" taken from *Past Imperfect*. Toronto, Ontario: House of Anansi Press, 2005. Used with the permission of the publisher.

"Ideal World" and "If You See It What Is It You See" taken from *The Irrationalist*. Toronto, Ontario: House of Anansi Press, 2010. Reprinted with that permission of the publisher.

"First World Problems A to Z" taken from *A Pillow Book*. Toronto, Ontario: House of Anansi Press, 2016. Reprinted with that permission of the publisher.

# Mark Callanan

"The Meaning of Life", "The Myth of Orpheus" and "The Ship" taken from *Gift Horse*. Montreal, Quebec: Véhicule Press, 2011. Reprinted with the permission of the publisher.

"Part of the Main" reprinted with the permission of the author.

# Chad Campbell

"Et In Arcadia Ego" and "Iain Lachlan Campbell" taken from *Laws & Locks*. Montreal, Quebec: Véhicule Press, 2015. Reprinted with the permission of the publisher.

"Hear Ye" taken from *Euphonia*. Toronto, Ontario: Anstruther Press, 2016. Reprinted with the permission of the author.

"The Fifth Season" reprinted with the permission of the author.

## Dani Couture

"Union Station" taken from *Sweet*. Toronto, Ontario: Pedlar Press, 2010. Reprinted with the permission of the publisher.

"Interview with the County Reporter" and "Salvage" taken from *Yaw*. Toronto, Ontario: Mansfield Press, 2014. Reprinted with the permission of the publisher.

"I Come Around with Appetite to Parties" taken from *Black Sea Nettle*. Toronto, Ontario: Anstruther Press, 2016. Reprinted with the permission of the author.

"Contact" reprinted with the permission of the author.

## Kayla Czaga

"Funny", "That Great Burgundy-Upholstered Beacon of Dependability" and "Victoria Soto" taken from *For Your Safety Please Hold On*. Gibsons, British Columbia: Nightwood Editions, 2014. Reprinted with the permission of Nightwood Editions, www.nightwoodeditions.com.

"Harvest Moon Lantern Festival" reprinted with the permission of the author.

## Sadiqa de Meijer

"Introducing the Incredible Pseudomorph", "Pastorals in the Atrium" and "Yes," taken from *Leaving Howe Island*. Fernie, British Columbia: Oolichan Books, 2013. Reprinted with the permission of the publisher.

"On Origins" used with the permission of the author.

# Joe Denham

"From *Windstorm*" taken from *Windstorm*. Gibsons, British Columbia: Nightwood Editions, 2009. Reprinted with the permission of Nightwood Editions, www.nightwoodeditions.com.
"From *Regeneration Machine*" taken from *Regeneration Machine*. Gibsons, British Columbia: Nightwood Editions, 2015. Reprinted with the permission of Nightwood Editions, www.nightwoodeditions.com.

# Raoul Fernandes

"Attachments", "By Way of Explanation" and "The Goodnight Skirt" taken from *Transmitter and Receiver*. Gibsons, British Columbia: Nightwood Editions, 2015. Reprinted with the permission of Nightwood Editions, www.nightwoodeditions.com.

"Self Storage" reprinted with the permission of the author.

# Autumn Getty

"Repose" and "Pender and Hamilton" taken from *Repose*. Gibsons, British Columbia: Nightwood Editions, 2008. Reprinted with the permission of Nightwood Editions, www.nightwoodeditions.com.

# Jason Guriel

"Empty Nests in Leafless Trees" and "Less" taken from *Pure Product*. Montreal, Quebec: Véhicule Press, 2009. Reprinted with the permission of the publisher.

"John Hancock's John Hancock" and "My Father's Stamps" taken from *Satisfying Clicking Sound*. Montreal, Quebec: Véhicule Press, 2014. Reprinted with the permission of the publisher.

# Leah Horlick

"Amygdala", "Anniversary" and "Little Voice" taken from *For Your Own Good*. Caitlin Press: Halfmoon Bay, British Columbia, 2015. Reprinted with the permission of the publisher.

"There Must Be A Name For This" reprinted with the permission of the author.

# Liz Howard

"Look Book", "Terra Nova, Terraformed" and "A Wake" taken from *Infinite Citizen of the Shaking Tent*. Toronto, Ontario: McClelland & Stewart, 2015. Reprinted by permission of McClelland and Stewart, a division of Penguin Random House Canada Limited.

"Euro—Anishinaabekwe—Noli Turbare" reprinted with the permission of the author.

# Stevie Howell

"Crunches", "A Girl's Will" and "Rip Torn" taken from *Sharps*. Fredericton, New Brunswick: Goose Lane Editions, 2014. Reprinted with the permission of Goose Lane Editions.

"Rain Pool" taken from *Summer*. Toronto, Ontario: Desert Pets Press, 2016. Reprinted with the permission of the author.

# Amanda Jernigan

"Aubade" and "Catch" taken from *Groundwork*. Windsor, Ontario: Biblioasis, 2011. Reprinted with the permission of the publisher.

"Beasts" and "Lullaby" taken from *All the Daylight Hours*. Markham, Ontario: Cormorant Books, 2013. Reprinted with the permission of the publisher.

publisher.

"Something softens me" taken from *I have to live*. Toronto, Ontario: McClelland & Stewart, 2017. Reprinted by permission of McClelland and Stewart, a division of Penguin Random House Canada Limited.

## Evan Jones

"Anteros", "The Horn Gate" and "Nausicaa" taken from *Nothing Fell Today But Rain*. Markham, Ontario: Fitzhenry & Whiteside, 2003. Reprinted with the permission of the publisher.

"God in Paris, 1945" and "Self-Portrait with Argus the Hundred-Eyed" taken from *Paralogues*. Manchester, Great Britain: Carcanet Press, 2012. Reprinted with the permission of the publisher.

## Sonnet L'Abbé

"Ah", "Killarnoe" and "Repetition" taken from *Killarnoe*. Toronto, Ontario: McClelland & Stewart, 2007. Reprinted by permission of McClelland and Stewart, a division of Penguin Random House Canada Limited.

"Brain Stem" taken from *Anima Canadensis*. Toronto, Ontario: Junction Books, 2016. Reprinted with the permission of the author.

"CXXVIII" reprinted with the permission of the author.

## Ben Ladouceur

"Armadillo", "I Am in Love with Your Brother" and "The Masturbating Flowers" taken from *Otter*. Toronto, Ontario: Coach House Books, 2015. Reprinted with the permission of the publisher.

"Vulgaris" reprinted with the permission of the author.

## Jeff Latosik

"The Piñata" and "Song for the Field Behind Mississauga Valley Public School" taken from *Tiny, Frantic, Stronger*. London, Ontario: Insomniac Press, 2010. Reprinted with the permission of the publisher.

"Foley Artist" taken from *Safely Home Pacific Western*. Fredericton, New Brunswick: Goose Lane Editions, 2015. Reprinted with the permission of Goose Lane Editions.

"The Internet" and "Mind" taken from *Helium Ear*. Toronto, Ontario: Anstruther Press, 2016. Reprinted with the permission of the author.

## Canisia Lubrin

"Keepers of Paradise," "The Mongrel" and "Voodoo Hypothesis" taken from *Voodoo Hypothesis*. Hamilton, Ontario: Buckrider Books, 2017. Reprinted with the permission of the publisher.

## Nyla Matuk

"Don Draper" and "Poseurs" taken from *Sumptuary Laws*. Montreal, Quebec: Véhicule Press, 2012. Reprinted with the permission of the publisher.

"Appetites", "I Declared My Ethnicity" and "Stranger" taken from *Stranger*. Montreal, Quebec: Véhicule Press, 2016. Reprinted with the permission of the publisher.

## Jacob McArthur Mooney

"A Guide to Getting It Right" taken from *The New Layman's Almanac*. Toronto, Ontario: McClelland & Stewart, 2008. Reprinted by permission of McClelland and Stewart, a division of Penguin Random House Canada Limited.

"Mapfolk" taken from *Folk*. Toronto, Ontario: McClelland & Stewart, 2011. Reprinted by permission of McClelland and Stewart, a division of Penguin Random House Canada Limited.

"The Fever Dreamer" and "Golf Pro, Monobloc, *A Theory of the Firm*" taken from *Don't Be Interesting*. Toronto, Ontario: McClelland & Stewart, 2016. Reprinted by permission of McClelland and Stewart, a division of Penguin Random House Canada Limited.

## Sachiko Murakami

"Portrait of Suburban Housewife as Missing Woman", "Skipping Stones" and "Wishing Well" taken from *The Invisibility Exhibit*. Vancouver, British Colombia: Talonbooks, 2008. Reprinted with the permission of the publisher.

"Rebuild" taken from *Rebuild*. Vancouver, British Colombia: Talonbooks, 2011. Reprinted with the permission of the publisher.

"They expanded the Icelandic-food-as-gifts store" taken from *Get Me Out of Here*. Vancouver, British Colombia: Talonbooks, 2015. Reprinted with the permission of the publisher.

## Alexandra Oliver

"Meeting the Tormentors in Safeway" and "Party Music" taken from *Meeting the Tormentors in Safeway*. Windsor, Ontario: Biblioasis, 2013. Reprinted with the permission of the publisher.

"Christopher Robin Kindergarten Class Photo, 1974" and "Plans" taken from *Let the Empire Down*. Windsor, Ontario: Biblioasis, 2016. Reprinted with the permission of the publisher.

## Soraya Peerbaye

"Disque" taken from *Poems for the Advisory Committee on Antarctic Names*. Fredericton, New Brunswick: Goose Lane Editions, 2009. Reprinted with the permission of Goose Lane Editions.

"Gorge Waterway" taken from *Tell: Poems for a Girlhood*. St. John's, Newfoundland: Pedlar Press, 2015. Reprinted with the permission of the publisher.

## James Pollock

"Radio", "My Grandmother's Bible", "Sailing to Babylon" and "Prague" taken from *Sailing to Babylon*. San Jose, California: Able Muse Press, 2012. Reprinted with the permission of Able Muse Press.

## Michael Prior

"Conditional", "Half", "Swan Dive" and "Ventriloquism for Dummies" taken from *Model Disciple*. Montreal, Quebec: Véhicule Press, 2016. Reprinted with the permission of the publisher.

"In Cloud Country" reprinted with the permission of the author.

## Damian Rogers

"Redbird", "Snake Handler" and "Song of the Last Shaker" taken from *Paper Radio*. Toronto, Ontario: ECW Press, 2009. Reprinted with the permission of the publisher.

"Good Day Villanelle" and "The Trouble with Wormholes" taken from *Dear Leader*. Toronto, Ontario: Coach House Books, 2015. Reprinted with the permission of the publisher.

# Johanna Skibsrud

"I'd be a Hopper Painting" taken from *Late Nights with Wild Cowboys*. Kentville, Nova Scotia: Gaspereau Press, 2008. Reprinted with permission of the publisher.

"I do not think that I could love a human being" and "Mast" taken from *I Do Not Think That I Could Love a Human Being*. Kentville, Nova Scotia: Gaspereau Press, 2010. Reprinted with the permission of the publisher.

"Come and See the Blood in the Streets!" taken from *The Description of the World*. Hamilton, Ontario: Buckrider Books, 2016. Reprinted with the permission of the publisher.

# Souvankham Thammavongsa

"Materials" and "Water" taken from *Small Arguments*. Toronto, Ontario: Pedlar Press, 2003. Reprinted with the permission of the publisher.

"At the Farm" and "Bare" taken from *Light*. St. John's, Newfoundland: Pedlar Press, 2013. Reprinted with the permission of the publisher.

# Nick Thran

"Seriously, It Was the Biggest Cricket" taken from *Every Inadequate Name*. London, Ontario: Insomniac Press, 2006. Reprinted with the permission of the publisher.

"Seven Cicadas" and "Earworm" taken from *Earworm*. Gibsons, British Columbia: Nightwood Editions, 2011. Reprinted with the permission of Nightwood Editions, www.nightwoodeditions.com.

"Mayor Snow" taken from *Mayor Snow*. Gibsons, British Columbia: Nightwood Editions, 2015. Reprinted with the permission of Nightwood Editions, www.nightwoodeditions.com.

## Daniel Scott Tysdal

"A►◄B (A MAD Fold-In Poem)" taken from *Predicting the Next Big Advertising Breakthrough Using a Potentially Dangerous Method*. Regina, Saskatchewan: Coteau Books, 2006. Reprinted with permission of the author.

"Last Poem", "Sonnet 155" and "The Walls" taken from *Fauxccasional Poems*. Fredericton, New Brunswick: Goose Lane Editions, 2015. Reprinted with the permission of Goose Lane Editions.

## Sheryda Warrener

"Through the Restaurant Window" taken from *Hard Feelings*. Montreal, Quebec: Snare Books, 2010. Reprinted with the permission of the publisher.

"A Sudden Gust" and "We Bought a Little City" taken from *Floating is Everything*. Gibsons, British Columbia: Nightwood Editions, 2015. Reprinted with the permission of Nightwood Editions, www.nightwoodeditions.com.

"Self-Portrait: *Cassiopeia 1*" and "Self-Portrait: *Nimbus II, 2012*" used with the permission of the author.

## Ian Williams

"Not Saying" and "Triolet for you" taken from *You Know Who You Are*. Hamilton, Ontario: Wolsak and Wynn, 2010. Reprinted with the permission of the publisher.

"He will tell me later the story of the woman he has been alluding to all day" and "Missed connections: Walmart automotive dept—w4m—(Lunenburg MA)" taken from *Personals*. Calgary, Alberta: Freehand Books, 2012. Reprinted with the permission of the publisher.

"Corrections" reprinted with the permission of the author.

## Catriona Wright

"Gastronaut", "Instinct" and "Yelp Help" taken from *Table Manners*. Montreal, Quebec: Véhicule Press, 2017. Reprinted with permission of the publisher.

# Acknowledgements

*Poetry* published a portfolio solicited from contributors to *The Next Wave* in December 2017. Many thanks to Don Share, Lindsay Garbutt, Holly Amos, Fred Sasaki, and all at the Poetry Foundation.

Thanks also to Shane Neilson and Katie Fewster-Yan for their editorial feedback on the introduction to this book.

# About the Editor

**Jim Johnstone** (b. 1978) is a Toronto-based poet, editor, and critic. He's the author of five books of poetry, including *The Chemical Life* (Véhicule Press, 2017) and *Dog Ear* (Véhicule Press, 2014). He's also the winner of a CBC Literary Award, *The Fiddlehead*'s Ralph Gustafson Poetry Prize, and *Poetry*'s Editors Prize for Book Reviewing. Currently, Johnstone curates the Anstruther Books imprint at Palimpsest Press, and is an associate editor at *Representative Poetry Online*.